THE GOLF MURDERS

THE GOLF MURDERS

A Readers' And Collectors' Guide
To
Golf Mystery Fiction:
An Annotated and Illustrated
Bibliography

Thomas F. Taylor

Golf Mystery Press
Westland, Michigan
1997

Published by Golf Mystery Press. Printed and bound in the United States by BookCrafters of Chelsea Michigan.

Publisher's Cataloging-in-Publication Data
(Prepared by Quality Books Inc.)

Taylor, Thomas F., 1936-

The golf murders : a readers and collectors guide to golf mystery fiction : an annotated and illustrated bibliography / Thomas F. Taylor.

200 p. 23 cm.

Includes index.

1. Detective and Mystery stories, English—Bibliography. 2. Detective and mystery stories, American—Bibliography. 3. Golf-Fiction—Bibliography. I. Title

Z2014.F4T39 1997 (PR830.D4 016.823'087208
QBI96-40846

ISBN 1-890223-00-X

LCCCN 95-095338

First Edition May 1997

To *Phyllis*

Table Of Contents

ACKNOWLEDGMENTS

The Golf Murders had it's origin as a modest list maintained for the author's collecting purposes. The list was just a tool used in the assembly of the collection. When the decision was made to expand the list into a book, eventually making it available to others, the relationship between the collection and the list was reversed. The collection became the reference material for the vastly expanded list, which was slowly becoming *"The Golf Murders"*.

At that point, suggestions and, consultation were sought from many. Joe Murdoch and Dick Donovan, both golf bibliography authors of note, were especially supportive of the project and of it's value to readers and collectors of golf and mystery fiction. Alastair Johnston, Leo Kelly, Bob Kuntz and Peter Georgiady, all with non fiction golf books to their credit, gave advice and encouragement.

A considerable number of the books featured were originally recommended by fellow dealers and collectors. Without their contributions, *"The Golf Murders"* would be noticeably thinner. Even then, despite the most persistent pursuit of needed titles, some never became available for inclusion. Thankfully, this same group of collectors and, dealers, came through with a number of color photocopies of dust jackets of books in their own collections, for the illustration section. There were a few cases, where collectors made such contributions to this work, conditioned upon confidentiality, a special thanks to those silent folks as well. There are many books which have completely eluded us. Certainly there also are titles which should have been included, of which we are not aware. Should a reader have information about, or access to any such title, please contact the author at the address at the end of the introduction. Sadly, the following acknowledgment list is incomplete. It was not uncommon, in an informal gathering of book people, for a new title to be suggested for inclusion. The name of the person making the suggestion was often not recorded. We are grateful to them and specifically to:

Robert Adey, Joseph Murdoch, Richard Donovan, Robert Kuntz, Alastair Johnston, Robert Smith, Leo Kelly, James Lay, Barry Pike, John Cooper, Richard Stewart, Hidetoshi Mori, Donald Ireland, Jamie Sturgeon, Rhod McEwan, Ralph Spurrier, Jack Adrian, Jim McArthur, Vickie Gibboney, Thea Clayton, Michael Mark, William Deeck, Charles E. Gould, Nathan Cushman, Ralph Elder, Marion Richmond, Jeffrey Meyerson, Andy Spisak, Marge Gartz, Darleen Curtis-Feasel, Ann Leonard, Angelo Plakas, Brian Siplo, Helen Olmsted, Loren Estelman, The Golf Collectors Society, and the British Golf Collectors Association

These authors generously responded to inquiries:

Keith Miles, David Williams, James Bartlett, W.R. Philbrick, Bob Jones, Nicola Furlong, David Hamilton, Robert Upton, Angus MacVicar, Conor Daly, J.M. Gregson, Paul Engleman, Ralph McInerny, James Ellroy, H.R.F. Keating, Charlotte & Arron Elkins, John Logue, John North, Rob Kantner and William Rocke.

The following references were used extensivly:

Doubleday Crime Club Compendium, Ellen Nehr, Offspring Press, 1992
Twentieth Century Crime & Mystery Writers, Leslie Henderson, St. James Press, 1991
Hawk's Author's Pseudonyms II, Pat Hawk
Crime Fiction II, Allen J. Hubin, Garland, 1994
Detective Fiction, 2nd, Pike & Cooper, Scolar Press
Artists In Crime, Cooper & Pike, Scolar Press
Encyclopedia Of Mystery and Detection Steinbrunner & Penzler, McGraw Hill, 1976
Contemporary Authors, Gale Research, Detroit
CADS, Geoff Bradley, Publisher
Publishers Weekly
The Armchair Detective

INTRODUCTION

"Do you have any golf mysteries today?"

I wish I had the proverbial nickel for every time I have asked that question. For more than 15 years, I've put that question to clerks and proprietors of new and used book stores. Hooked on mysteries, golf, and good books, not necessarily in that order, I have spent a big chunk of my life slaking my thirst for good golf mysteries.

Most often, the clerks answer would be a regretful "Sorry, no." The number two answer was usually: "Oh, do you mean like *Murder on the Links*?"

Ah, yes, Agatha Christie's *Murder on the Links.* Published in 1923, it is the best known golf murder mystery, and one of the highest priced today. It fetches well over $5,000 in its first edition with original dust jacket — if one can be found for sale. Most such copies are in private collections. Dedicated readers and collectors like us, will most likely never get a chance to see one, much less possess one.

During these past 15 years of collecting golf mysteries, I picked up many facts like these — things that can be valuable to you in your collecting:

- Christie wrote 5 other full length mysteries, that contain golf— more golf than *Murder on the Links.*

Golf also figures in three of Christie's short story mysteries.

- Christie clearly was somewhat ambivalent about the game. This may or may not have been influenced by the fact that she lost her first husband to a woman with a better handicap.

These are the kinds of facts you will find in the pages of *The Golf Murders.* You'll find many interesting snippets and little known facts about the world of golf mysteries:

- Eight authors (in addition to Christie) published golf mysteries whose titles differ between their American and British editions.

- Many golf mysteries have no tell-tale golf terms in the titles and no giveaway golfing illustration on the dust jacket.

- Paperback originals can be very collectable. Example: James Ellroy is a highly acclaimed author of mystery–detective stories. His first was a golf mystery titled, *Brown's Requiem.* First published in paperback in the U. S., then published in England in hardcover.

More than a bibliography, more than a dry listing of titles and publishers. *The Golf Murders* is a treasure trove of facts and opinions about, nearly 200 mysteries with golf in them. Most are wonderful reads, and there are a few certifiable dogs. Most are full length hardcovers, some are paperback originals, and others are short stories. Some are recent, many old, a few are extremely rare. Whether you are a bookstore employee, rare book dealer, librarian, collector, or garden variety golf / mystery fan, you will find *The Golf Murders* to be a valuable resource. It is also, to the extent that I could make it, an enjoyable reading and browsing experience.

But *The Golf Murders* is, most of all, a labor of love.

The largest known collection of golf mysteries

It started with a love of mystery fiction. Nothing beats a good mystery — an intriguing crime, a baffling set of clues, an intrepid investigator, peril, danger, and a satisfying (and sometimes thrilling) payoff.

To that add a love of golf. Being obsessive and in a position that allowed for it, I played a lot. Never well, but a lot! And, being a reader, I sought out books on golf to help improve my game. At first it was instructional books, then biographies of famous players. Finally, came some terrific golf fiction: P. G. Wodehouse, Bernard Darwin, and others.

Having discovered golf fiction, I now sought out mysteries with golf themes. The supply seemed terribly limited. To help in the search, bibliographies were consulted. In particular, two terrific general references for the golf book collector—reader were utilized.

Joseph Murdoch, co-founder of the Golf Collectors Society, authored a bibliography titled *The Library of Golf,* published in 1968 by Gale, Detroit. This landmark book, is now itself, much sought after as a collectable. It lists almost a thousand titles, and specifies those that Murdoch considers to be important, for the serious golf book library to contain.

Richard Donovan then authored (with Murdoch collaborating) another terrific bibliography, *The Game of Golf and the Printed Word,* Castilo Press, Endicott, NY, 1987. It lists, by time period, 4800 golf books. It gives publisher information only: author, title, publisher, date and place of first and subsequent editions.

All of this was wonderful information and all of it was helpful, but very few of the books listed were golf mysteries. Several standard mystery bibliographies were checked, each including a handful of golf titles, but that was all. One, called *Murder by Subject,* under sports, listed about 15 golf mystery titles.

Of course, there had to be more than these. One thing noticeable about the golf–mystery titles in these mystery bibliographies was, the books all had the word golf in the title or a golf illustration on the cover. There certainly had to be a number of mysteries with golf settings that did not have such telltale giveaways. Two such examples are Ian Fleming s *Goldfinger,* and *Fer-de-lance* by Rex Stout. These are classic golf mysteries, but the titles and covers contain no golf hints.

So it was clear, if more golf mysteries were to be found, they would have to be found the hard way, one by one. Starting with, my then small list, I began visiting used book stores, mystery fairs with book exhibits, and other venues. When a mystery, with a golf setting was turned up, I first tried to find more books by the same author, figuring that an author who had once used golf in a mystery, might do it again in other titles. But finding these — if they existed — was often a challenge. Sometimes the newly found book was published 60, 70, 80, or more years ago, often there was no dust jacket. Sometimes it was not possible to tell if the author was British or American, if the book was first edition, or a reprint, or if the author had ever published anything else.

First, off to the local mall bookstore, where the clerk would go blank, when the computer turned up nothing. Next to the local library card catalog or computer system. There, I found, more often than not, was only the title of the book which started the search in the first place.

Continuing the quest, I haunted used book stores, used book fairs and shows, always asking questions, pestering collectors and dealers, corresponded with authors, and, like a good detective, pursued every lead in search of golf mysteries. The search extended to visits with dealers and shops all across North America, as well as in Britain and Europe. Stacks were searched in small town libraries and the Library of Congress in Washington, D.C., and a number of golf museums.

Book by book, the list and collection grew. The search uncovered golf mysteries by well known authors and, obscure ones, series writers, one-shot wonders, hardcover and paperbacks, novels and short stories, British and American. Mysteries were found, saturated with golf, and others in which golf was just a minor element.

As the collection grew, the list was continually updated so as to avoid accidentally buying something twice. That list also grew and grew, and became the basis for this book. Now the collection is, without question, the largest known collection of golf mysteries. *The Golf Murders* is my effort to share this special collection with all golf–mystery fans.

In choosing titles for this book, the standards applied were very subjective, and flexible.

If a book sold in the *mystery* (or, in England, *detective fiction*) area of the bookstore, then it is classified as a mystery. As to the amount of golf necessary to make it qualify as a golf mystery, that was impossible to quantify. If we erred, it is on the side of inclusiveness.

Generally, the golf sequences needed to have some relationship to the plot, or to illuminate the characters in some way. So, if the story only includes one swing at a golf ball, but the impact of that swing causes a poisonous dart to shoot out of the club handle into the player, thereby killing him, that would be enough to qualify the book as a golf mystery. On the other hand, if the book includes a large number of golf sequences that can be lifted out without affecting the plot or informing us about the characters, then the book is not a golf mystery. Twenty of these so-called non-qualifiers, but still good reads with some golf connection, have been gathered in a special section called: These Didn't Make The Cut!

What you will find in *The Golf Murders*

Section One lists over 160 full length books and 24 short stories, alphabetically by author and then by title. Each entry includes:

Factual information about the author (including pseudonyms), publisher, date of first edition, place of printing, physical size of the book, number of pages.

A detailed review of the book. This includes a description of the amount and type of golf in the story, a brief summary of the plot (without giving away anything!), and a purely subjective opinion of the book in terms of readability and entertainment.

The second section contains color illustrations of dust jackets. Most of these are from books in my personal collection. Special permission was also obtained to include photographs of some especially rare dust jackets from other collections.

The third section includes indexes and a number of special lists and cross-references. The titles are listed in the following ways.

Alphabetical by title

Type of mystery (cozy, soft, or hard-boiled)

Gender of author

Gender of protagonist

Country the book is set in.

Type of golf content:

Professional–Tour (PGA or LPGA) or

a friendly game or competiton.

So as not to spoil the endings, there is no listing of the titles by the type of murder weapon used. So far, while no story has been found in which the murder was committed with a ball washer, all the following have been utilized.

- Exploding ball
- Exploding club head
- Explosive charge in the cup
- Exploding golf course—No kidding!
- Speared with the flag stick
- Trick club
- Bloody golf club
- Sabotaged golf cart

Finally, there is a list of paperback originals (printed only in paperback, or the true first edition was in paperback).

The future of golf mysteries

The good news is that there are, at present, at least seven authors producing a golf–mystery series. Combined with the individual efforts of non-series writers, we have lots of great golf fiction to look forward to.

The bad news is, that despite exhaustive searching, *The Golf Murders* is probably not complete. So if you enjoy a good golf mystery, or maybe even those that are not so good, I have a request. Please, send me your comments, your criticisms, and (most especially) the titles of golf mysteries , and color copies of dust jackets if possible.Your contributions will be gratefully acknowledged.

Golf Mystery Press

P. O. Box 85396

Westland, Michigan, 48185

Chapter 1

Novel Length Golf Mysteries

Adams, Herbert, British, 1874 - 1958, *Jonathan Gray*,

Herbert Adams wrote mysteries for more than thirty years under his name and as Jonathan Gray. Among them were eight novel length golf mysteries, seven as Adams and, one **The Owl**, as Gray. Adams also wrote a collection of golf short stories, titled **The Perfect Round.** Most of the stories in **The Perfect Round** are light comedy, much resembling Wodehouse's tales by *the oldest member.* One, is a mystery, and it has been included in our short story section. The stories here by Adams all contain at least one murder. In all these stories, Adams used golf, chiefly match play and mixed foursomes, to reveal character strengths and flaws of the players. Golf games advanced both romances and murder investigations. The actual golf sequences are described with affectionate detail. He sometimes created heated discussions, among players and bystanders, regarding fine points and strategies of the game, particularly match play.

The underlying mysteries and the golf are as fresh as anything written today. This probably accounts for the resurgence of collector interest in Adams' work, especially in Britain and Japan, where the cozy style mystery tale is preferred. The golf titles, except for **The Golf House Murder** are difficult to find, some nearly impossible in their first edition dust jackets. Most have not been reprinted.

THE SECRET OF BOGEY HOUSE
Methuen, London, 1924, 252 pages, 18 cm

Lippincott, Philadelphia, 1925, 252 pages, 19.5 cm

Tony Bridgeman came out of W.W.I. a hero. He invested his soldier's bonus, and his inheritance, all of his money, into a new high flying insurance company. Then he treated himself to a vacation at a golf resort. The last day of the vacation, he learned that the insurance company had gone bust, and so was he. Deciding to worry later, he went out for a last round of golf, a poor shot put his ball into the shrubs bordering a home at the fairway's edge. While probing under the bushes his luck changed, he looked up to find a lovely young woman watching him. They talked, she soon introduced Tony to her guardian, who recognized him as having been an amateur golfer of some status before the war. The old fellow offered Tony a job, as his nephew and a large amount of cash were missing. The nephew was last seen at a golf resort known for its gambling called Bogey House. Tony was to check in, gamble at golf and bridge, and find the nephew. He was fitting in at Bogey House when the nephew was found murdered. Tony's task was now to find the killer! When not playing golf, he poked around Bogey House, finding hidden passages leading down to a boat house, which contained a speed boat capable of crossing the channel. He soon was uncovering smugglers and art thieves. Toward the end there is a wonderfully described car chase, involving the vintage cars of the day. There's a good bit of golf. The story is pure entertainment.

THE GOLF HOUSE MURDER
Lippincott, Philadelphia, 1933, 313 pages, 19 cm
JOHN BRAND'S WILL
Methuen, London, 1935,

Susan Heriot, a beautiful young heiress, returns to England from a vacation in the West Indies. She found that her adopted father (who never formally legalized her adoption) had died. His brother, and the brother's two children, have seized the house. They produce a will, executed by the dead man a few days before he died, which leaves everything to them. Susan turns to her late father's lawyer. He had drawn up the original will that made her the sole heir. After examining the new will, he sadly tells her that it appears to be in order. Watching this is the lawyer's son, himself to be a lawyer shortly, and he is smitten with Susan. They team up and investigate. Their plan to talk with the family chauffeur is foiled when he is found dead in the golf house, of the club of the bad uncle!

As is the case in Agatha Christie's **The Murder On The Links**, the body being found on a golf course, (or in this case, in the club house) is the only golf connection in the story. **The Golf House Murder** version has a golf illustration on the dust jacket, but there is not a single stroke played. This is a typical Adams story. A cozy murder counterpointed with a sweet romance, and a cast of clearly defined evil, and virtuous characters.

THE BODY IN THE BUNKER
Collins Crime Club, London, 1935, 244 pages, 19cm
Lippincott, New York, 1935,

Members of the Barrington Golf Club were assured the enjoyment of its golf course and the tranquil company of similar fellows in the card rooms and salons of Dormey House. Much as a hotel, Dormey House offered rooms to members wishing accommodation. A few, like Bill Broughley, a bachelor of simple tastes and ample means, made it their principal residence.

The normally placid atmosphere was shattered by an ugly quarrel between two members in the card room following dinner. It was witnessed by most of the members, on hand for the beginning, next day, of the annual Captain's Prize golf matches. In the morning, the first group of contestants on the course found one of the previous night's antagonists dead in Hell Bunker, at the short fifteenth. The dead man, Crosbie, was considered by most members to be generally disagreeable. Quickly, a determination was made that this was murder! The police soon heard of the near fight in the card room. They learned that Broughley, the other party in the altercation, left Dormey House the night of the murder. He was later seen walking the road which ran within a few yards of the fifteenth green and the sixteenth tee. Investigation revealed blood stains at the sixteenth tee and, that it was possible to fall, or be pushed off the tee and down into

Hell Bunker. In Crosbie's pocket was a note, requesting a meeting at the sixteenth tee, at 10 pm, the time of death. The note's author, a lovely young woman, lived across the road from the sixteenth tee, and could see it from her window. She denied knowledge of the note, until it was found she was the divorced wife of the dead man. Under pressure, Broughley admitted that he was very friendly with the lady. Adams delivers the usual match play golf and fine story we expect from him.

DEATH OFF THE FAIRWAY

Collins Crime Club, London, 1936, 283 pages, 18 cm

The reader is witness to a murder in the first chapter. How it's committed is revealed, but absent is the *Who* and the *Why*, and it's the last chapter before all's made clear.

Roger Bennion is playing golf, mixed doubles, with two recently met pretty young women, and his male friend, Carol. On the backside of the course, a small river borders the fairway on the right, to the disconcertion of the slicer. Roger drove straight and far and Carol, striving to follow, sliced toward the river. While the foursome hunted Carol's ball, Roger, seeing a body in the river, walked into the waist deep water and pulled it onto shore. The reader knows that the victim, Basil Shelton, was murdered, but the local police and two doctors, make it suicide. Roger can't stay out of it and soon finds that Shelton, recently retired and of independent means, had bought his house on the bank of the river opposite the course just ten days before. He then made arrangements with his pretty niece to come live with him. Why kill himself, and if he was determined to do it, would he drown himself in a cold little river, only waist deep? The niece arrives and is adamant in her rejection of suicide. Shelton's will, made in the last few days, leaves all to her.

It first seemed that Shelton was a total stranger to the area. Then first one, then another, until there were at least three local residents who had past dealings with him. All these affairs resulted in bad feelings, but, bad enough to commit murder? During all this, another Adams trademark, romances being furthered by frequent mixed partner golf matches, is going on. The mystery, romances, and especially the golf are all delightful.

THE NINETEENTH HOLE MYSTERY
Collins Crime Club, London, 1939, 252 pages, 19 cm

Roger Bennion is Herbert Adams' favorite amateur detective and here again he is in one of the golf mysteries. **The Nineteenth Hole Mystery** starts with Bennion checking in at the Allingham Golf Club and Resort, in Dorset, for a planned week on the links with a friend. Arriving, he finds his playing partner has been forced to cancel. Being a friendly fellow, he soon meets a foursome of men who are also away for a week of golf and is asked to join in their matches. Before long, another member from the home club of this foursome appears at Allingham, and in quick order, he is murdered. The foursome, Bennion's new friends, all had their own reasons for despising the victim. So to, it turns out, a few locals who each had a connection to him. Soon following, the clubhouse barman who everyone seemed to like, is murdered. The police are completely mystified. Bennion, who can't resist a murder, involves himself in the case and, is very helpful to the local constabulary. They need the assistance, but resent him none-the-less. There's a lot of golf, most being match play and mixed four balls, between couples. The golf is what we expect of Adams, well played and intelligently described. The story, not having suffered from sixty years passing, provides a good read.

This is one of the few of Adams' golf mysteries which has been reprinted. The reprint seen, was a paperback edition having the original dust jacket art work on its cover. The reprint appeared to be from the 1950's and is now as scarce as the first edition in its dust jacket.

ONE TO PLAY
Macdonald and Company, London, 1949, 244 pages, 19cm

Roger Bennion, driving in the highlands beyond Inverness, stops to assist a stranded lady motorist. She is traveling with two small children, twins, and is very secretive about who they are and where they're going. He gives her some fuel and off she goes. Returning to London, he finds a message from a friend pleading for his assistance in solving a murder. The lovely, single female author of the request, clinches her appeal by telling him to bring his golf clubs, as her father would love to play him again. Presumably, the clubs are already in the car, the light bag with only seven clubs, as he is immediately en route to help.

At Fairway, Kesselton, Cheshire, Joan Abbott greets him with a kiss and her story. Her young friend Beatrice, had married Gerald Challen; twice her age and a beastly man, and after three years of marriage he divorced her. On false evidence he gained custody of the couple's twin girls. Six days later he was murdered and Beatrice and the twin girls disappeared. Bennion learns that Beatrice is a scratch golfer and often represented the local club in mixed foursome matches away from home. Her golf partner was named the corespondent in the divorce and he is the main murder suspect.

After meeting the local police investigator and assuring him he wouldn't meddle, Bennion has Joan schedule golf games with persons who benefit from Challen's death. He had immediately realized that the stranded motorist was Beatrice and, he first dashed back to the highlands and persuaded her to bring the twins and, return with him. Soon back, and continuing his golf playing investigation, he is nearly killed on the course when the killer becomes convinced he is getting too close.

The story reads like a contemporary novel, fast, tight, and smooth. A few false leads lend interest and the killer isn't revealed until the final page. The golf is integral to the plot. It's all match play, fondly described. Our favorite Adams!

DEATH ON THE FIRST TEE
Macdonald and Company, London, 1957, 192 pages, 19cm

Publisher's blurb, taken from the inside front flap on the dust jacket.

"I would rather go to your funeral than to your marriage with that man!" Lady Darlington's angry retort to the news that her pretty daughter Monica was planning to marry a fellow member of the Greenham Golf Club did not indicate a dislike for the royal and ancient game or those who play it. Her concern lay solely in the fact that the member of Monica's choice was Obobo, the son of a native chief in a British Colony. Others at Greenham already showed resentment over Monica's preference for the dusky visitor; not least her brother, Gerald, who saw in it a possible threat to his own marital ambitions. Then, in a mixed foursomes' competition, Death played a round and claimed a victim on the first tee. Roger and Ruth Bennion were among the competitors, and when Inspector Yeo was detailed to find the murderer he asked Roger to assist him. Action must be swift and decisive, for on the outcome might hinge the destiny of a whole people

There's a second murder at the golf club before it's over. A lot of golf is talked about but little played. Race relations are discussed in the manner of the day. Much has changed in the past forty years. Written near the end of Adams' career, this is the last of his golf mysteries.

Allen, Leslie H, 1887 - 1973 , *Horace Brown*

MURDER IN THE ROUGH

Five Star Mysteries, Inc., # 45, New York, 1946, Paperback original, digest size

Boardman, London, 1948, Paperback, using his pseudonym, Horace Brown.

The publisher's blurb from the back cover.

When Napoleon B. Smith drove his golf ball into the rough of Hell's Half-Acre, he had not the slightest idea that he was headed into a jungle trail of murder that would tangle

him with one of the most ruthless killers of his long career as a criminologist.

In this swiftly paced murder mystery you will meet a detective who will certainly become one of your favorite fiction sleuths: Napoleon B. Smith. Mastodon of a man, grim and ruthless as any killer, a private investigator who learned about crime the hard way — on the police beat. And you will chuckle over the wisecracks and love affairs of his writing sidekick, Leslie Allen.

If Nero Wolfe got out of the house and played a little golf he would resemble Napoleon Smith. In addition to their physical make-up, and wise-cracking sidekicks, they both maintain a rocky relationship with the local police.

There's not much golf, but Napoleon has such a terrible slice that you have to feel for him. He knows he will never play well, but he will not stop playing. The writing is a little dated, but the story is interesting enough to keep you reading to the finish.

Anderson, W.A.

KILL 1 KILL 2

William Morrow & Co., NY, 1940, 284 pages, 19.5 cm

The exact time and location of this story is never stated. Somewhere in the mountains of upstate New York or Pennsylvania in the late 1930s would probably be pretty close.

Wealthy industrialist, James Gennitt, built an enormous lodge in these mountains two years ago. The workers were still putting in the swimming pool with its water piped in from a nearby stream. Gennitt's idea of a vacation at the lodge involved taking his family, personal secretary and, all the staff required for him to continue to run his empire. On this trip he had invited another utility company owner, his wife and son to the lodge. There were rumors that Gennitt was planning a takeover of his guest's company and he was trying, without success, to assure him it wasn't true. Gennitt left the lodge early in the morning, on a short business trip. He was driving himself so that he could be alone and think. That was the last time he was seen alive. The car was found wrecked, off the road, unoccupied. The police searched unsuccessfully, but it was the lodge's Indian gardener who found the body. An unexplained head wound, looked like it could have been made with a golf club, so the local police confiscated all three sets at the lodge. The golf course used by guests is less than a mile from the lodge. Gennitt's vice president, his personal secretary and the son of his apprehensive competitor are all golfers and were out that morning. The vice president aspired to move up. The secretary ran things much of the time and he liked the power. The competitor's son feared the loss of his life style, should his father lose their company. The final solution involves the layout of the golf course and its proximity to the lodge. There's talk of golf and some chipping and putting practice in the lodge hallways.

This one is very difficult to find in first edition with the paperback reprint being only slightly easier.

Ball, Brian; *Brian Kinsey-Jones, B.N. Ball,* British

DEATH OF A LOW-HANDICAP MAN

Walker and Company, New York, 1978, 224 pages, 21 cm.

Barker, London, 1974, 224 pages, 21 cm.

Set at *the finest course in industrial Yorkshire*, so, sayeth the members. It also seems to be a pretty fair place to commit murder. The first murder takes place in "the spinney", a wooded rough just off the first fairway. The discovery of the body, accompanied by disconcerting shouting, took place exactly as a member, who happened to be a policeman, was hitting his drive off the first tee. Victim number two was pushed from the club house roof at midnight. (What was he doing up there?) This, while the club president was making presentations to the winners of the annual Irish Match.

The Irish Match starts, with all able members drinking as much as they can, on the president's tab. When the president determines that sufficent inebriates have been consumed to level out the members' handicaps, he takes the sodden lot of them to the course. There, they tee off, en masse. The object is not to play the golf holes, but rather to play all the way across the course, without regard to hazards, roads, buildings, etc. It is a feat to survive crossing the course, which now resembles an artillery range. There is likely to be a couple of golfballs rocketing by a player at any given moment. The winning score last year, shot by the aforementioned policeman member, was seventeen. The Irish Match is only a small segment of the story. There is much about the fondness the members feel for their club. The policeman is under a terrible strain, conducting a murder investigation, in his club, among his friends. Well written. There is a lot of very, very unusual golf.

Bartlett, James Y., US,
DEATH IS A TWO STROKE PENALTY
St. Martins Press, New York, 1991, 181 pages, 21.5 cm

While this is the author's first book, he has been writing about golf for national publications for ten years. So too, his protagonist, Peter Hacker.

Hacker is a golf writer for The Boston Journal and follows the tour, from just outside the ropes. Hacker has unusual (unlikely) access to the players. He was a touring pro and lost his card. Not because of the shots he hit, or missed, but because he used a foot-mashie, (cheated) and got caught. Still, fifteen years later, he kibitzes with the pros and likes to beat balls on the practice range, as a way to work through vexing problems.

Hacker is covering a tour event in South Carolina when a rising young pro is killed. The young star was driving a golf cart at night, on a strange course, and drove it right off a bridge. It landed in the bottom of a ravine, on top of him. Even though the victim was always described as a *straight arrow*, there's an almost instantaneous rumor of drug use. The rumor is vehemently denied by his young widow, and she, in desperation, asks Hacker to investigate what is being brushed off as a tragic accident. She isn't buying it! She wants Hacker to look into the mysterious unofficial chaplain of the tour's "God Squad." Things aren't all serene, or, divine. Among the interesting characters who will not make the sports pages are a sweet hooker who likes golf and a drug dealing caddie. Before the tournament's over, the caddie is murdered.

This is one of the best, a satisfying story with plenty of golf, competitively played. There is also a lot of golf and tour talk, both in the locker rooms and bars.

DEATH FROM THE LADIES' TEE

St. Martins Press, New York, 1992, 195 pages, 21.5 cm

Peter Hacker, former tour player and current golf writer for The Boston Journal, is back. This is the second by a good writer, who actually knows golf, especially the pro tours.

Hacker is on vacation and bored when he gets a call from Honie Carlton, the *girl next door*, from his childhood. Now Ms Carlton, recently graduated with a marketing degree, is the P.R. Flack for the Ladies' Tour. It seems the ladies aren't getting enough good press and/or T.V coverage. T.V coverage (sponsors) are where the real money is. Her job is to generate interest in the LPGA and she's looking for a knowledgeable writer to do a puff piece as part of her promotion plan. Hooker is enlisted and flies to Doral to do the piece at an ongoing LPGA event. The plane tickets, hotel room, and sundry extras are all paid for by the players' association. Hacker's initial interview with Wynonna 'Big Wyn' Stilwell, former tour star and association president, sours immediately. She lists what, and what not, he's to write. His journalist ethics are offended, he becomes ticked, vociferous and fired in rapid order. He decides to write an exposé on Wyn and the way she runs things. Hacker talks to Benton Bergermister, Tour Commissioner. Benton talks when he drinks, but that stops with his death, an apparent suicide. Then Honie is severely beaten by persons unknown. Hacker picks up information about Big Wyn taking advantage of some of her young and very innocent players, in ways that they are ashamed to talk of. A good story. Golf, murder and sex, straight and otherwise, contribute to making Hacker's second outing a success.

Bentley, E(dmund) C(lerihew), British, 1875 - 1956

TRENT'S OWN CASE

A. A. Knopf, New York, 1936, 324 pages, 19cm

Constable and Company, London, 1936, 314 pages

This story does not have much golf, but it is critical to the plot. The style is a little dated, but Bentley, based on his three novels and one collection of short stories, (see *The Sweet Shot* in the short story section) is reputed to be one of the all-time best, and the story is interesting enough to see it through. Co-authored with H. Warner Allen.

Philip Trent, gentleman detective, is a wealthy portrait painter who knows everyone. A successful amateur detective from the right social class, he is welcomed by Scotland Yard on some of their tougher cases. A very wealthy philanthropist, James Randolph, is murdered in his London home shortly after meeting there with Trent. The next day, Trent is called in on the case because he may have been the last person to see the victim alive and, because he is such a big help to the police. The chief suspect is Dr. Bryan Fairman, recently fired from his position at a hospital that Randolph supported. Trent knows Fairman and, is sure he is innocent, even when presented with a handwritten signed confession.

The investigation reveals Randolph as a tyrant who controlled his staff with coercion and blackmail. His valet and his office manager, victims of his domination, are on the list of suspects. A lovely young actress who complained about unsolicited letters from Randolph is discovered to be his niece, and as he died without a will, she makes the list.

Randolph's son, who had left home at eighteen, turns up at police headquarters. He has no problem convincing anyone of his true identity because he is an exact, younger double for his murdered father. Certainly he has a motive.

Golf comes in when Trent takes his main suspect for a round at his home course. The suspect plays off a five handicap so Trent asks for three strokes. Trent is very cool. They are all even after the front nine holes.

Borissow, Michael, British,
THE NAKED FAIRWAY

Cranbrook Golf Club, Cranbrook, Kent, England, 1984, 192 pages, paperback original,

The following is from the back cover of this elusive title.

Baz Norton; who came up from the swamp to face a terrible threat as he challenged for supermacy in the maelstrom of the world's top pro golf.

Laura; The flame-haired lovely whose claims on Baz were so much over par.

Charlie; The old pro whose secret drove him to the brink of extinction.

Marie; Whose virginity led Baz towards a path of self-destruction.

Jaycee; Multi-millionaire boss of the golfers' jet-set.

Brenda; Whose appetites and jealousy made her cruelly vindictive.

Marco; The poisonous intruder into the multi-million dollar finances of the pro circuit.

All these vivid characters, plus the on and off-course dramas in the top flight of professional golf, expose the charisma of the world's greatest players.

Box, Sidney, British, 1907 - 1983
ALIBI IN THE ROUGH

Robert Hale, London, 1977, 176 pages, 19 cm

A good crime story built around golf. Without golf, the story's bank robbery would have been impossible to pull off. The robbers play a few holes, drive to town and hold up the bank, and then return to the course to finish their round. Would that put you off your putting stroke? The golf sequences are accurately done, and all too identifiable, for high handicappers.

Publisher's blurb from the dust jacket:

Why did four respectable, comfortably off and apparently carefree businessmen suddenly decide to rob a bank in their own town? And how did a golf foursome on their favorite course provide them with an unbreakable alibi? Unbreakable, that is, until a pretty girl was found dead on the ninth green, and a good family man who had lost his No. 4 iron committed suicide.

Alibi In The Rough is a thriller with a difference. It provides readers with a do-it-yourself kit for a bank robbery and a new way of using a golf course as a short cut to 100,000 pounds. When the men's wives enter the picture and husband-swapping is added to the hazards, the game gets rougher. At which point it is just as well to have an alibi-in the rough.

Only printed in England, this is getting to be a difficult title to find, but worth the effort.

Bream, Freda, New Zealand,
SEALED AND DISPATCHED
Robert Hale, London, 1984, 157 pages, 19 cm

Set in New Zealand, this series features The Reverend Jabal Jarrett, golf-playing suburban Anglican vicar, with a flair for solving violent crimes. There is not a lot of golf in the story, and although not essential to the plot, golf is important to understanding Jabal and his relationship to golf partner Terry. The descriptions of local scenes, customs, and speech patterns are interestingly done. Auckland, New Zealand, sounds like a very neat place.

One of Jarrett's regular golf partners, Terry Walton, is the fourth partner in the firm of Barley and Binns, Barristers and Solicitors. When the senior member of the firm is found murdered in his office, stabbed to death with the knife still stuck in his neck, Terry's first thought is that now his name will move up one on the list on the letterhead. He suppresses this unkind thought, because Terry is a kindly man.

During a round of golf, Terry attempts to engage Jabal in the case. Not to solve the murder, but to assist Smithson, another of the firm's partners, who seems to be the victim of blackmail. Between shots, Terry and Jabal discuss blackmail in general, and Jabal's slice in particular. Jabal agrees to see Smithson following the round, but the meeting accomplishes little, due to Smithson's lack of candor.

A few days later, a second murder takes place at the law firm. The victim is brained at his desk, with a heavy notary seal, while the staff is at a birthday party. The police determine the victim was Smithson's blackmailer, making him suspect number one. Jabal agrees to spend a couple of weeks working at the firm to see if he can solve the crimes. He is slow getting off the mark, and meanwhile there are two more attempted murders of the firm's staff.

THE VICAR INVESTIGATES

Robert Hale, London, 1983, 160 pages, 19 cm

Jabal's assistant has an aunt who runs a boarding-house in Rotorua, the geyser (hot springs) town of New Zealand. One of her guests has been found drowned in her spa pool, and in spite of police assurances, she is convinced that it was not an accident. Jabal is persuaded, by the pleas of his assistant and *the lure of Rotorua's golf courses*, to spend his forthcoming vacation investigating the death. Jabal's investigation technique involves daily rounds of golf with fellow boarding-house lodgers, who are also high on the list of murder susspects. There's a couple more killings before it's over and no real golf to speak of. A quick read with a lot more interesting stuff about this land on the other side of the world.

Bruff, Nancy, US, 1915 -, Nancy Bruff Gardner
THE COUNTRY CLUB
Bartholomew House, NY, 1969, 339 pages, 21.5 cm

This is certainly one of the quirkier stories in this collection, but it is also one of the more interesting. There is a lot of golf talked about and some played, and all of it is central to the plot.

Surmount Country Club maintains that it is the best damned golf course in Fairfield County. Many of the women members would also maintain that it has the sexiest golf pro on the Eastern seaboard. His name is Dunbar, and his apartment is located exactly above the women's locker room. "What could be handier?" suggests a leading female member. The Country Club, with its cold martinis and hot showers, is a hotbed of sizzling gossip. But all this was before conversation focused on the death of the club treasurer, who was found at the bottom of the empty swimming pool in his swim trunks.

Conversation does not linger on any one subject at Surmount Country Club. There are just too many juicy things, all supposedly secret things, going on. The club pro is giving golf lessons to lady members, on and off the fairways but not to the club's lady champion. She is golf crazy, loves the club, and hates the pro. She hates him so much that a grudge match is scheduled between them, with the loser agreeing to leave the club.

The men's champion is trying to work a real estate deal that would see the course sold to a land developer for a housing project. Five people, all connected with the club, die in suspicious fires. A couple of members know who is responsible but are not talking, for their own reasons. The reader also knows the killer's identity. Suspense is sustained because it is unclear if the killer knows who knows about him. When he finds out, will he kill again?

Burton, Miles, 1884 - 1964, British, *Cecil John Charles Street, John Rhode*
TRAGEDY AT THE THIRTEENTH HOLE
Collins Crime Club, London, 1933, 252 pages, 19 cm

This novel may well be the most elusive title of all the old golf mysteries. It appears to have been published only by The Collins Crime Club, London, with no U.S. printing. Neither a first edition of the book, nor any version of the dust jacket has been seen. The following publisher's blurb was taken from the front free-end-paper:

Mr. Burnside, a wealthy manufacturer, was playing a round of golf with his nephew on the links of Heavenbeach. He played his approach to the 13th, then walked with his caddie towards the green. He disappeared into the dip in which the hole lay. A few minutes later he fell dead, struck on the temple with a golf ball.

Well, accidents, of course, will happen on even the best regulated golf courses, but-Inspector Arnold has chosen Heavenbeach as a suitable spot for a quiet holiday and he was mildly puzzled by the apparently insignificant fact that three golf balls were found on the green. The Inspector invites his old friend, Desmond Merrion, to join him, and together they investigate The Tragedy At The Thirteenth Hole, which is certainly one of the most ingenious problems that the fertile imagination of Mr. Miles Burton has devised.

Bush, Christopher, (Charlie Christmas Bush) British, 1888-1973, *Michael Home*
THE CASE OF THE GREEN FELT HAT
Henry Holt, New York, 1939, 261 pages, 19 cm
Cassell and Company, Ltd., London, 1939,

Ludovic Travers was well known to readers in the 1940's. He was the main character in over fifty of the author's books. The story is set in England and, is a classic British cozy mystery, with sanitized violence and romance at arm's length while appealing to the reader's intellect. It has some good golf and an excellent story. The alibi of a central figure is based on his ability to fade a tee shot around a dogleg right hole while avoiding the trees on the right.

In this one, Ludovic and his new wife, are honeymooning in the quiet town of Edenstrope. They are enjoying the golf at Pettistone and the company of their friends, the local police chief and his wife. This peaceful scene is shattered when one of the local residents, with a notorious background, is found dead under a pile of refuse in a burning shed, near the golf course.

Travers, an unofficial expert whose help has enabled Scotland Yard to solve so many difficult murder cases feels compelled to assist his friend, the police chief. So a murder investigation is worked into the honeymoon and golf vacation. Besides, Travers is a writer of detective fiction and this could be grist for the mill.

Cake, Patrick, US, 1935 -, *Timothy L. Welsh*
PRO-AM MURDERS
The Proteus Press, Aptos, CA, 1979, 285 pages, 20.5 cm

This book is sprinkled throughout with gray, hazy photographs of the type taken using long-distance surveillance cameras. A number of the photographed scenes are of recognizable California landmarks. Pebblebeach, the Seventeen Mile Drive, Spy Glass, famous amateurs, and a number of beautiful women are featured. If you don't let the macho sex and the gimmicks drive you away, you will find some good golf here. I bet you'll finish this strange book.

Omnipotent, an evil organization, has developed a laser type of weapon of enormous power. Omnipotent is looking for a foreign government to buy this killing device, and they arrange a demonstration. They make a school bus, a driver and 24 children, disappears without a trace.

The authorities are convinced that the driver and kids are dead, and they don't have a clue as to the identity of the people behind Omnipotent. They contact Univest, which is not a brokerage firm, but a private anti-terrorist firm specializing in tidying up very dirty situations.

Dion Quince, the number one cleaner-upper at Univest, is authorized to do whatever it takes to stop Omnipotent. He quickly learns that Omnipotent has planned another demonstration for some interested buyers. This one will be on national television. The plan is to wipe out the final round of the Crosby Pro-Am golf tournament held on the Monterey Peninsula.

Quince is a last-minute entry in the tournament. He's a four handicap without practice, and he takes two days to sharpen his game. He is a James Bond type, single, handsome, and deadly. He kills without remorse, but only the bad ones. He gets to decide who the bad ones are and gender is irrelevant. Of course, there are lots of beautiful women in this story and some are equally lethal.

Canning, Victor, British, 1911 - 1986, ***Alan Gould***

THE LIMBO LINE

Heinemann, London, 1963, 254 pages, 20cm

William Sloane, NY, 1964, 288 pages, 21cm

There is not a lot of golf in this story, but it is an interesting element. The action moves across Europe like a James Bond movie. Lots of activity and no problem distinguishing between the good and bad guys.

Richard Marston had been quit of the British Secret Service for a couple of years when, during a friendly round of golf, his old boss tries to get him back for one more job. It seems that Russian defectors are disappearing from England and reappearing in their old home towns in Russia. They are all nonpolitical defectors; dancers, business people, sports figures, and the like. Why do the Russians even want them back, and how are they being spirited out of England and across Europe?

The Good Guys have obtained information on who will be the next defector to be grabbed. Irina is a dancer and beautiful. Marston meets her and, as his old bosses had hoped, is smitten. He agrees to take the case. She is, unknowingly, the hook to pull him back into the service. Neither is she told that she is to be used as bait to catch the Russians. The plan fails. She is grabbed and everything goes very wrong.

In the late stages of the story is another golf match. Marston and Company blow it and the Bad Guys pull off another caper. The story moves along and has a satisfying ending.

Causey, James O., US,
KILLER TAKE ALL

Graphic Publishing Co., NY, 1957, 157 pages, Paperback

Robert Hale, London, 1960, 160 pages, 19 cm

This is a rather unsuccessful attempt to copy Mickey Spillane, mitigated with some good golf sequences.

Tony Pearson returns to his job as a country club golf professional after a disastrous first attempt at competing on the pro golf tour. While he's been gone, his girl friend, with whom he fought about trying the tour, has married. Her husband is big and tough, smart and handsome, and very wealthy. Tony grabs a kiss from his old girl friend and the new husband decks him.

Tony stews, lets the situation interfere with his job, and, understandably, gets himself fired. Then the husband, who has now beat Tony physically, taken his girl, and won at chess(huh?), offers him a new job. The husband is opening a new, very plush golf club, and offers Tony the head pro position there. Tony suspects he may be getting set up, but, he will do anything to stay close to his old flame.

His fears are confirmed when he is accused of stealing an oil painting from a secret room in the new club house. The painting was one of a collection of oils by old masters. Tony's boss is just the custodian for the collection, which is part of the treasury of the mob. It is suggested that some of the paintings are fakes and the theft was a cover-up to keep the mob bosses from confirming the fraud. Three murders follow in rapid order, with Tony the main suspect in all of them.

Besides the mob, stolen paintings, the girl friend, and murders, there's golf. Tony's boss is hooking the ball but does not want to change his swing. He challenges Tony to straighten out his shots without messing with his swing. Tony tinkers with the bosses driver, adding lead tape and changing sole weights. The ball flies far and sure. Righttt!

Chabody, Philip & Florence, US,
THE 86 PROOF PRO
Exposition Press, Jericho, NY 1974, 184 pages

Anyone who has ever hit a great tee shot, put the second shot right in front of the green, and then taken five more to get down, will love the golf in this story.

This story features the Las Vegas Open, with probably more currency riding on it than sponsor Howard Hughes might imagine. The stakes run even higher with tension mounting, as life and death are wagered and a round of golf is transformed into a game of Russian Roulette.

Ed Dunnum is in charge of a top-secret ABM program, but after an information leak to the Russians, Ed is hastily and unjustly fired from his $150,000-a-year job. Before picking up the pieces of his life and starting over, Ed and his wife, Gloria, decide to have a fling in Las Vegas, with the exciting roll of the dice and the jangling bells of the slot machines to add some color to their rather gray-tinged future.

The scene of a grandiose golf tournament sponsored by Howard Hughes, in Las Vegas, acts as a magnet, drawing golfers, celebrities, and of course, hustlers from near and far. And with $100,000 going to the winner, three professional gamblers (Frank, Harry, and Wayne) conjure up a scheme to rig the Vegas Open and win a bundle. Their enthusiasm for this scheme has apparently over-ridden their natural caution, as it requires the ripping off of the mob's bookmakers. The mob is noted for having a very low tolerance for rip-offs, of *their* money.

The rancor Ed feels against the establishment that ostracized him outweighs his better judgment, as he allows himself to be wooed into taking part in the computerized caper.

The three hustlers pick Don Fletcher, "The Bob Hope Of The Fairways," as the golfer on whom to bet their bankroll, regarding his weakness for alcohol as an asset for their purposes. The dubious honor of caddying goes to George "Mother" Goose, a good-hearted little guy, but a born loser in the game of life. He sees this scam as his chance to be on easy street for a long time.

Christie, Agatha, British, 1890 - 1976, *Mary Westmacott*

The most popular writer of fiction of all time, her 80 plus full length books have sold well over 500,000,000 copies. She continues to sell well today. Her first husband, Archibald Christie, loved golf and she played some. Their first home was selected for its proximity to a new golf course. Archibald eventually divorced Agatha and soon after married a pretty young lady with a lower handicap. Agatha is not recorded to have played golf after the divorce, but the game figures in five full length and a number of her short story mysteries.

THE MURDER ON THE LINKS

Dodd, Mead, New York, 1923, 298 pages

John Lane, London, 1923, 298 pages

The *Murder On The Links* is the most famous of the golf mysteries. It is also, by far, the most expensive in first edition. It is rare and pricey because, as it is only her third mystery, written early in her career, the first edition was printed in modest numbers, and Christie is aggressively collected, all over the world. Over 70 years old, this title makes it into *The Golf Murders* solely on the basis of its author's reputation and the golf title, not the golf content.

Hercule Poirot, a former Belgian police detective, is retired and living in London. He is in a class by himself for the application of the *little gray cells* to unsolvable cases. This reputation keeps him in demand as a private detective.

Poirot receives in the mail, an urgent summons from a terrified man in France, requesting his help. He arrives too late and finds his prospective client murdered. The body has been dumped alongside a shallow grave on the property behind the man's estate. This property is being developed into a golf course. The grave was dug in the loose soil of an as yet unfinished bunker.

WHY DIDN'T THEY ASK EVANS?

Collins Crime Club, London, 1934, 252 pages

THE BOOMERANG CLUE

Dodd, Mead, New York, 1935, 290 pages, 20.3cm

With more golf in it than in any other Christie book, this classic British cozy mystery is full of twists and turns. Bad shots are described with such detail, it convinces the reader that the author had first hand knowledge of the experience.

The story begins with a round of golf between the local vicar's son, Bobby Jones, and a doctor friend. A fiercely attacked niblick shot by Jones, slices off the course, over a steep cliff, and down to the beach. Trying to recover the ball, Jones comes on a dying man who appears to have fallen over the cliff. Just before the man dies, he opens his eyes, looks straight at Jones, and asks the question which gives this book its British title.

The doctor goes for help in removing the body. Jones, left with the body, sees a photo sticking out of the man's suit pocket. Pulling it out, he looks at a photo of a very lovely young woman. At the inquest a few days later, a much different woman appears and claims to be the sister of the deceased.

The next day, young Jones is playing golf on the same course with the vivacious daughter of the local Lord. She is eager for all the details of the incident, and he gives them to her as they play. She attended the inquest which ruled accidental death, and is dissatisfied with this finding. The young couple decides to investigate further, and they are very resourceful in their quest. This couple provides all the love interest likely to be found in a Christie.

TOWARDS ZERO

Dodd, Mead, New York, 1944, 242 pages, 20 cm

Collins Crime Club, London, 1944, 160 pages, 19 cm

This is a typical Christie in that there are false leads and double backs. Of course it is a good read, as you would expect of an author who has sold a half billion books. There is no golf played, except perhaps at a murder scene in a bedroom. This seems to be the only golf mystery by Christie which has a golf illustration on the first edition dust jacket. The Collins printing displays an iron club lying across holiday party paraphernalia.

Lady Camilla Tressilian will host the yearly gathering of the family at Gull's Point. Only this year there is a problem. Nevile Strange's former wife Audrey and his current wife Kay will both be there. Kay is sure that no one likes her and that she is only tolerated because she is Mrs. Nevile Strange. But they must go because elderly Camilla, Nevile's aunt, holds in trust an estate that will go to Nevile and his wife upon her death.

Things go badly from the start. Mr. Treves, a very ripe and experienced eighty, and a good old friend of Camilla (as well as her lawyer), dies of a suspicious heart attack after an evening with the group at Gull's Point. Shortly, Camilla is found dead in her bed. Her head has been bashed in, and a bloody niblick is on the floor.

The police are called and find that the blows, if they were done with this golf club, would have required a left handed, upright swing, utilizing an overlapping grip, open stance, and out-to-in club path. This swing pattern does not fit any of the people in the house, and so the mystery continues.

WHAT MRS. MCGILLICUDDY SAW

Dodd, Mead, New York, 1957, 192 pages, 21 cm

THE 4:50 FROM PADDINGTON

Collins Crime Club, London, 1957, 256 pages, 19 cm

Agatha Christie's other detective, Jane Marple is "a dithery, fluffy octogenarian" and a terrific deducer of criminal facts! There is not much golf in this story, but, it is an element of the plot.

When Jane's friend, Elspeth McGillicuddy, arrives for a visit and says that she just witnessed a murder, Jane gives her tea while they discuss the details. Elspeth, riding on a train, recounts how she saw a man kill a woman in another train as the two trains passed. She immediately reported what she saw to train personnel, who grew more disbelieving when a check was made and no body found.

Jane does not doubt her friend and so determines that the body must be found to get the police believing. She enlists the assistance of another extremely competent woman to do the ground work. Lucy Eyelesbarrow is Oxford trained but prefers to work as a supercharged domestic. She takes a position in the household of an estate that borders the railway, in an area where Jane thinks the body was thrown off the train.

Lucy brings her clubs along to her new position, and goes looking for the body in her off time by deliberately mis-hitting chip shots into bushes, ditches, and fences along the tracks. In the course of the investigation, two more people are murdered. Once Lucy has collected her facts, Miss Marple sets a trap for the killer and invites the police.

Cooney, Caroline B., US, 1947 -
SAND TRAP

Avon Books, New York, 1983, Paperback

This story is set in the Sandhills area of the Carolinas, where golf is an industry and the golfing visitor is catered to. There are golf scenes, actually, there are golf flashbacks, played out in the mind of the killer. The book is a quick read, with a good ending. This is a paper-back original with a wonderfully sinister golf illustration cover.

The main character, Janney Fraser, a fortyish lady, seems to be without the strength to carry on after her husband walks out on his family. Without a word or a note, he has left both her and Ross, his war-crippled son by a previous marriage. The bedridden Ross hates being alone while she works and, resents the burden he is to her when she gets home and, must bath and care for him. Janney, an accomplished musician, is trying to make ends meet as an organ demonstrator - seller in a music store. There is little glamor left in playing organ requests all day long for bored shoppers who feign an interest in purchasing an organ as a way of killing a few minutes. The store is in a shopping mall, a lenghty drive from her home. She works long hours, often well after dark. She actually looks forward to the long drive home at night as driving in her car is the only time she has all to herself.

Late one night, on her way home through the back country, and completely absorbed in private thoughts, she drives by a murder in progress on the shoulder of the road. She is so engrossed in thinking about her problems, she does not see a thing. However, the killer thinks she did.

The killer chases, she runs. She comes to find that she is much stronger than she would have believed, and the reader will come to admire her resourcefulness. Nearing her home the killer closes in on her and she tries to hide in a small church where she plays the organ for Sunday services. The killer follows. Out of the church and across the golf course which separates it from her home, goes the deadly game of hide and seek. The local and the state police, the crippled stepson, the killer and his aunt, and the lady organ player turned very-uncooperative-victim, all end up on the golf course, or in the sand trap.

Cork, Barry, British

This author sold his first short story at age sixteen and has served on the staff of several British magazines. More recently he was president of Fleetway Publications in New York. He and his wife live in Norfolk, England. This splendid golf mystery series features Angus Struan, golfing policeman.

DEAD BALL

Charles Scribners, New York, 1989, 220 pages, 21cm

Collins Crime Club, London, 1988, 220 pages, 22 cm

Angus Struan is a highland born Scot. A good enough amateur golfer to qualify for *The Open*, he decided to become a policeman rather than try the pros. He now plays to a ten handicap because his left shoulder was almost blown away a few years ago by a bank-robber with a shotgun. The police administration kept him on because he's very good with paperwork. The desk was bad enough, but, then his wife left. To busy himself, he writes about his other interest, English long bows and armour. He knows a lot about their history. He writes a historical novel, sells it and buys a Maserati. Now he's working on his second book, which is already sold, and he's thinking about chucking police work altogether.

While on leave, he's asked to visit a neighboring golf club which is setting up to host a pro event. Someone has plowed up the first green and threatening more destruction if the tournament isn't canceled. A turf consultant is found in a bunker with a broken neck. When Angus gets back to his home he finds that a thirteenth century crossbow is missing. One of the crossbow's missiles (bolts) impales a pretty golf tour public relation flack to a tree in Angus' front yard. While visiting him, she went out in the rain, wearing his rain coat and hat, to get cigarettes out of his car. The crossbow accounts for another kill, almost in Angus' arms before it's over. Angus ends up a caddie for the final thirty-six holes. There are some quite nicely done golf sequences and this is a fine start to a welcome new series.

UNNATURAL HAZARD

Charles Scribners, New York, 1990, 176 pages, 21cm

Collins Crime Club, London, 1989, 176 pages, 22 cm

While visiting an auction, looking for antique weapons, armour, and related old stuff, Angus runs into a former golfing friend. The friend was a famous American tour pro who has moved to the west coast of Scotland and bought an island. On the island is an authentic castle with lots of history. The new owner is turning the castle into a hotel and the whole island into a golf resort. As a way to kick off this project and get some publicity, the owner is staging a pro-am golf event with a number of big names. There's an opening and he invites Angus to come on up and play. Angus accepts, not just for the golf, but to see the castle and it's infamous oubliette. A oubliette is a secret dungeon from which, prisoners once thrown, never return. Arriving at the castle after most of the other guests, he gets introduced around. Once settled, he sets off to explore the oubliette. Looking down into the dungeon, with the aid of a strong light, Angus sees something that is definitely not an antique. There is a body at the bottom! Retrieved, it turns out to be another of the pro-am guests. The event is delayed, but not canceled, and finally gets off. Another guest walks, or is pushed, off a cliff in a heavy spotty fog during the match. In addition to the golf, very well done, there's treasure diving off a Spanish Armada ship. There is a particularly nice golf match on the mainland between Angus and an elderly gentleman. It figures neatly into the story. Two up for Cork!

LAID DEAD

Charles Scribners, New York, 1991, 183 pages, 21cm

Collins Crime Club, London, 1990, 183 pages, 22 cm

The writing is going well. Angus now has sold three historical novels. He has acquired a literary agent, who is his lady friend, and, serious? romantic interest. Things are looking up at the police job as well. He's been reassigned to London CID in recognition of his good work with terrorists (Dead Ball). This state of euphoria cannot last. First he gets a call from his ex-wife, asking for his help with her current male friend. He says he will try to help and this ticks off the girl friend/literary agent. The ex-wife sets up a meeting over golf at a local country club. The ex's boy friend does not show and Angus decides to salvage whats left of the day with a game of golf with another member he knows. There's a terrible accident on the next tee. A man is struck in the head with a driver by his playing partner, who, of course, is the ex-wife's boy friend.

Over the next day-and-a-half the pro shop is looted and, shortly after, the pro is murdered. To top off this whole mess, the powers-who-be assign it to Angus. The Home Office has gotten involved because the ex-wife's boy friend is from Holland and a special person to the British government. The action is swift, with con games, very tricky car bombings, fast and super expensive cars, and golf. Golf in both England and Holland. Then all hell breaks loose when the six year old son of Angus is snatched from the ex-wife. Cork just keeps getting better.

ENDANGERED SPECIES

Charles Scribners, New York, 1992, 176 pages, 21cm

Collins Crime Club, London, 1992, 176 pages, 22 cm

Working on a new book, Angus takes some time off to do research. He's traveling the way he likes best, driving his Maserati. His son and Laurie Wilson, the literary agent—girl friend are with him. They are on a back road in a remote corner of Lincolnshire when the Maserati breaks down. A local farmer who thinks he is directly descended from the Saxons befriends them. He puts them up in his guest house and arranges to have the car repaired by a crew of aircraft mechanics. These guys are rebuilding a circa 1940 B-24 in a nearby hangar of what was a World War II, USAAF bomber base. The car requires a special machined part and these fellows have the tools and the skills to make anything. It will take a few days, so they may as well relax and enjoy the restful countryside. An American, formerly stationed at this base, returns for some golf and a little nostalgia. He's shot in the head. The next day, one of the mechanics, diving in a lake off the end of the remaining runway, drowns. Day three finds Angus playing a round of golf with an eighty year old, former British Open Champion. The game ends when his electric powered golf trolley is destroyed in a bomb blast. All of it makes sense after a while and, there's is a good bit of interesting golf worked into the plot. The reader will also learn something of the renovation of vintage aircraft.

WINTER RULES

Charles Scribners, New York, 1993 192 pages, 21cm
Collins Crime Club, London, 1991, 192 pages, 22 cm

Now, that he is more or less permanently assigned to the London Police department, Angus has the time to work on his golf game and the handicap is down to eight. Laurie Wilson, literary agent—girl friend and he are semi-permanently living together. He treats himself to a new Maserati and in short order it's stolen. He would have preferred to never see it again, as to see it smashed up, the way it was found. The department assigns him to the new crime wave, the theft of luxury cars for shipment to African countries. Then the British Foreign Office requests Angus be made available to a visiting African President, who happens to be golf crazy. These requests are really orders and Angus soon gets picked up at his home in the President's Rolls Royce for the trip to the country club. They get shot at while on the course and, returning to the club house, find that the Rolls Royce has been stolen. Mysteriously, it is recovered and returned, intact. After some British golf, the President asks Angus to visit his country and inspect the golf course he is building. It will be the first in that part of Africa. The Foreign Office is ecstatic about the idea and suggests that perhaps Angus can learn something of the route of the stolen luxury cars which are flowing out of England and into Africa. Angus goes to Africa and tries some snooping around and gets shot at again. This time it's a heavy machine gun. The bad guys are playing a loose set of *winter rules*. There is less golf in this fifth Angus Struan than the others, but a lot of talk of building courses. There is also a lot about the international trade, with the complicity of some governments, in stolen vehicles. Another good story.

Crawford, Ian, Scotland, 1922-
SCARE THE GENTLE CITIZEN
Hammond, Hammond, London, 1966, 224 pages, 19cm

Despite winning some prestigious tournaments, his golf brought him nothing but fame, because he played as an amateur rather than a professional. His other love, writing plays, brought in very little cash because as yet his plays had only been done in Scotland. To keep it all going he accepted writing assignments for a Glasgow newspaper and cranked out features articles. The most recent was about ten unsolved murders in Glasgow. The police were upset to have their failings back in the news but, the real problem for Ewan Moray, writer, was that one of the ten killers believed he had new information that could lead to an arrest.

The killers broke in on an intimate house party he was attending and shot his host to death. Ewan, convinced that he was the real target, had his susspicions confirmed a couple of nights later, when he was attacked, knocked unconscious, stripped naked, driven to a remote location and thrown into a pitch black basement. Once again conscious, and fumbling around in the dark, he put his hand on a decidedly female breast, equally naked. The lady turned out to be another of the ill fated party guests. After a little mutual fondling, just to keep their spirits up, they escaped and hid in the nearby woods. By daylight, Ewan determined they were in the neighborhood of a golf course he knew. While breaking into the pro shop and stealing clothes they learned from the shop's radio that they were both wanted by the police for two new murders, at which articles of their clothing had been found. Fearing both the police and the killers, they set out to solve the case and clear themselves.

Ewan's golf celebrity helped in the solicitation of assistance, although he was required to give a chipping lesson, during a lull in the investigation. Golf is sprinkled throughout this story, which seems to be the only mystery published by the author.

Cruickshank, Charles, Scotland, 1914 - 1989
THE TANG MURDERS
Robert Hale, London, 1976, 182 pages, 19cm

There are four qualifications for membership in Gaydon Heath Golf Club. You must be stinking rich, well connected, live on the abutting estate, or be a bloody good golfer.

The newest member, Jack Griffin, is all four! He has just purchased Okanagan, a twelve acre estate whose eastern boundary runs alongside the whole four hundred and seventy yards of the daunting par four, twelfth hole. This geographical fact along with a stretch of frontage on a terrific trout river had some bearing on bachelor Jack's decision to buy the eight bedroom house, with heated pool.

Though well bred, educated, a scratch golfer, and expert fisherman, no one had a clue as to the source of his wealth. The last, and seemingly, only available records showed him recently to have been clerking in a low paid government office. But he's just paid two hundred thousand pounds *cash* for the estate.

Within an hour of taking possession of the house, Jack has a run-in with an angry neighboring millionaire on the golf course. Then events got much more serious. The mansion next door is burgled and the butler murdered. Stolen was a priceless collection of Tang Horses and Riders, antique Chinese ceramics of the highest order.

Jack meets and, is quite taken, with the lovely daughter of the neighbor who lost the priceless horses. She involves Jack in the search for them. This is made more difficult because the owner, having reported the burglary and murder, will not tell the police about the stolen ceramic collection. There quickly follows three more murders. Jack, being in the area of each of the murders, is a prime police suspect. Finally, watched by millions of BBC television viewers, Jack brings the killer to book after a dramatic chase at the Gaydon Heath World Golf Championship. Cruickshank, a member of Royal Wimbledon GC, knew his golf!

***Daly, Conor*, US, Pseudonym of Kevin Egan**

Like his series character, the author is a New York native, former caddie and an attorney. During the 1980s he was a member of the Rye Golf Club, played twice a week and his handicap fluctuated between 10 and 15. Since 1990 he's only getting in a couple of rounds a year and usually breaks 90. Look up his short story, **Pulling The Hagen**, published under his real name, in the short story section.

LOCAL KNOWLEDGE

Kensington Books, New York, 1995, 258 pages, 18.5 cm

Kieran Lenaham wasn't born *Shanty* Irish but his becoming a lawyer was more than was expected from a poor kid in Milton, New York. He practiced law for a few years and was good at it and, then chucked it to become a professional golfer. When he didn't make it on the PGA Tour, he happily accepted the job of head pro at Milton Country Club. There he practiced, grooving his swing, and entering local events. His golf game peaked, winning the Metropolitan Golf Championship, on the same day one of the founding members of his home club was murdered on his course.

Sylvester Miles had been hit in the head with a pitching wedge and his body thrown in the pond near the eighth green. Miles was a genuine W.W.II War Hero, who stayed on in Germany during the occupation. The wedge that pitched him into the beyond was manufactured in Germany, during the war by a golf crazy Nazi industrialist who created special *wonder-clubs* for Hitler's foursome. The wedge and the rest of the set would bring six figures at an auction of golf collectibles.

Lenaham increases his practice time, because his local win qualified him for the Classic, a New York State PGA event. His tune up schedule includes running the proshop, hitting balls during the day, and investigating the murder at night. He gets a terrific beating from unknown assailants just after he uncovers a plan to sell Milton Country Club to a Japanese golf resort company. There's some discussion of the business of golf collectibles, especially clubs which had been owned by an historical figure. There's also lots of golf played, and some golf course design. A good series start.

BURIED LIES

Kensington Books, New York, 1996, 258 pages, 18.5 cm

Kieran qualified for the PGA championship! After six years of playing local tour events he won one and now he's getting ready to go to Winged Foot for the PGA. His game is in good shape and he has a caddie, Jackie Mack, who is just magic — on the golf course. Jackie can take a course yardage book and edit it into a literary classic. He adds prevailing winds, fairways slopes, and innocent looking spots that should be avoided like the plague. Should Jackie's golfer find himself in one of these spots, there's cryptic instructions in the margins on the smart thing to do to recover. With a sweet golf swing and Jackie Mack on the bag, Kieran is ready for the big guys and Winged Foot.

Of course that situation can't last. First it's the pro shop. It gets torched and is a total loss. The fire inspector calls it arson and Kieran's insurance won't pay off. The members whose clubs were in the storage room aren't covered either, and they are jerked! The golf carts in the attached barn were destroyed and the loft where a dozen foreign caddies lived, also burned. As soon as it was safe to enter the burned out building, Kieran crawled through the Fire Marshall's yellow tape - looking for some personal mementoes, his first trophy, won as a caddie and a framed and personally inscribed picture of Arnold Palmer. They were gone!

The next day Kieran got the news that Jackie Mack jumped, fell, or was pushed in front of the Amtrak Train at the Milton Station that morning. Kieran's ex-wife says she saw two men running from the station platform just after Jackie's fatal dive. The police quickly make it a suicide and won't look for the two guys. The local priest won't give Jackie, a suicide, a funeral mass. Jackie's mother asks Kieran to talk to the priest. The police arrest Kieran for arson and murder. Murder because a firefighter died when an explosion in the cart barn fire killed him.

Out on bail, Kieran must get his trial date changed because it's set to start the second day of the PGA. On opening day, Kieran goes to Winged Foot and shoots a new, competition-round, lifetime low score. It's a complicated story with lots going on, that ties up neatly, and the golf is superb!

Daly, Elizabeth, US, 1878 - 1967
UNEXPECTED NIGHT
Farrar & Rinehart, New York, 1940,
Victor Gollancz Ltd, London, 1940, 223 pages, 19 cm

This is the author's first book and it introduces Henry Gamadge, book and autograph expert and amateur detective extraordinary. The book has one golfing sequence. It also talks a good deal about summer stock theater, make-up, and creating illusions. The writing is a bit dated, but the story is interesting, with a great twisted ending that repays the reader.

The plot revolves around young Amberley Cowden, who inherits a million dollars on his 21st birthday and is found dead, just hours later. There are more murders and bodies pile up quickly. Henry Gamadge, with the acquiescence of the local police, is allowed to involve himself in the case.

As the case develops, Henry instructs a couple of the female murder suspects to pick out their favorite golf club and join him in playing a fun round on the local resort golf course. Henry and the ladies walk the almost deserted fairways, hitting shots and enjoying the fresh air. As they stand on the green of a short hole, a ball hit from the tee behind them streaks through their group, nearly hitting them. They turn to look back, and no one is there!

Convinced that someone had just tried to kill one of them, they quit playing. As they walk toward the club-house and past the practice tee, they observe a powerful woman golfer, who is also one of the suspects, booming drives with deadly accuracy out onto the range.

The first edition of this book, like many first books by an author who becomes very collectable, is scarce and in dust jacket is rare. Happily, it has recently been reprinted by Otto Penzler in a paperback, which features the original dust jacket art on it's cover.

***Devine, Dominic*, Scotland, 1920 - 1980, pseudonym of David McDonald Devine**
THREE GREEN BOTTLES
Collins Crime Club, London, 1972, 224 pages, 20 cm
Doubleday Crime Club, NY, 1972, 221 pages, 21.5cm

The author, an attorney, worked much of his life at St. Andrews University. He lived in the town and, was a member of the Royal and Ancient Golf Club and, the St. Andrews Bridge Club. He wrote a number of mysteries, but this is the only one with a golf connection. It features three killings, all on an unnamed golf course, but not a stroke of golf. More the mystery, given the author's background.

The dust jacket blurb reads,

When a pretty girl is found strangled on the golf links, and shortly after, the junior doctor in a local partnership, a young man with a history of nervous instability, is found dead at the foot of a cliff, the police are satisfied that they know the identity of the murderer. Only two people are not: the young man's brother, and the writer of an anonymous letter which asserts that the young doctor was pushed.

In an effort to clear his brother's name, Dr. Mark Kendall takes his brother's place in the partnership, and is soon drawn into the social circle of the senior doctor. This includes the doctor's much younger second wife; their retarded daughter; Dr. Ben Radford, the family's close friend; the earnest daughter of the doctor's first marriage, at odds with her stepmother; and the attractive schoolteacher to whom Mark's brother had been engaged.

When a second schoolgirl dies and it is obvious that Terry Kendall was not the murderer, all these people react in an unexpected way. Through the skillfully interwoven narratives of the various characters, the reader follows events, until the death of a third girl brings into the open the bold and cunning murderer.

Dexter, Ted, and Clifford Makins, British
DEADLY PUTTER
George Allen & Unwin, London, 1979, 151 pages, 22 cm

This story contains as much or more good golf as any golf mystery we know of. Some matches are played for high stakes, which the players put up, and some are played for glory. It is all described in a style of which Darwin would have approved.

This book is difficult to find, despite being a relatively recent publication, but the search is certainly worth the effort. These same two authors did only one other book, a cricket mystery titled **Testkill**. Both these author's were sportsmen of note in Britain, with Dexter being the most famous. Dexter, nicknamed "Lord Edward" had been both the Captain of the England Cricket XI and a very useful competitive golfer as well.

The Putter, or, more properly, *The President's Putter,* is a golf match played in January each year at Rye, in England. The match is open only to the former members of the Cambridge golf squad.

This year's entries include former classmates Jack Stenton, a British gentleman sportsman; Rodney South, brilliant golfer, using drugs to get through the days; and Phil Beckermann, an American businessman who is trying to duck out on partners in the Mafia. Each man is fifty years old, and this is the last time any of them can expect to have a real chance to win The Putter.

Before the match, the players have a couple of days to warm up or, more correctly, to get accustomed to playing in the cold of winter. South and Beckermann have a blood match to settle, so after a practice round in which everyone holds back and sandbags, a high stakes match is set.

During the golf, wonderfully detailed, several murders are committed. To further muddy things up, an errant hit-man kills the wrong golfer.

Dickson, Carter, British, 1905 - 1977
John Dickson Carr, *Carr Dickson, Roger Fairbairn*
MY LATE WIVES
William Morrow, New York, 1946, 282 pages, 19.5 cm
Heinemann, London, 1947, 222 pages, 19 cm

Dickson had the superstar status of a John Grisham during his time, and the story is well told, but somewhat dated. There is almost no golf played in the story, but golf is critical to the plot.. The killer is not revealed until the very last. The following is taken from a dust jacket blurb:

All Roger Bewlay's wives had four things in common. No near relatives-a hunger for romantic love-an idyllic honeymoon-and, after their honeymoon, nobody ever saw them again. A great killer, an artist at his profession-until the doughty gentleman, Sir Henry Merrivale, lumbered on stage, golf club in hand, murder in his heart as he stalked a golf ball-and a mad man.

Four women disappear following their honeymoons, and the police consider them to be murder victims. The crimes go unsolved, with no leads, for eleven years until an unknown author writes a stage play about these murders. The anonymous script contains facts known only to the police and the killer. A famous British stage actor, to whom the play is delivered, decides to act out the script. He takes a month off and journeys to the town mentioned in the script as the place where the killer would come out of retirement and strike again. Sir Henry, ardent golfer and amateur detective, invites himself along, and the game is afoot!

Dods, Marcus, Scotland, 1874 - 1935
THE BUNKER AT THE FIFTH
William Hodge and Company Limited
Edinburgh & Glasgow, 1925, 186 pages

Some golf is played early in the story. Additional talk of golf clubs and the location of a body in a bunker make this a classic golf mystery. The dialog is dated, but the story is interesting, with some surprising twists at the end. This is a scarce one, and in it's original dust jacket, it must be classified as rare.

Alan Graham invites a business acquaintance, Mr. Seymore, to his club for a weekend and to fill out a golf foursome with two other friends. The three are members at Burnfield Clubhouse near the town of Brunton. The course is on the Firth of Forth and is home to The Worshipful Society of Edinburgh Golfers. Needless to say, it is very, very exclusive.

The golf is going great, and Alan is especially enjoying a few days away from his important staff position with a very powerful government commission. However, the commission decides to move the resumption of its deliberations up a couple of days, and Alan receives a telegram, directing him to be in attendance.

On Sunday evening, he tells the group that he will be taking the morning train to Edinburgh and then on to the commission headquarters. As the walk to the train station parallels the golf course, he will carry his clubs and play the first five holes.

Alan gets away first thing in the morning. A bit later, the remaining members hear that Seymore has been found dead in the bunker at the fifth hole. He has a large gash in his head, and Alan's niblick is lying nearby. A little later, a note signed by Alan is found in the shack of the club's handyman. The note implicates Alan in the death.

Alan's two friends are truly unable to tell the Edinburgh police inspector where he has gone off to. The newspapers are full of "The Body in the Bunker," and the search is on for Alan.

DuBois, William, US, 1903 -

THE CASE OF THE DEADLY DIARY

Little Brown, Boston, 1940,

THE DEADLY DIARY

Macdonald, London, 1947, 223 pages, 19 cm

This little gem of a book was first spotted as a possible candidate for inclusion in The Golf Murders because of a tiny dust jacket illustration on the book's spine. A broken wodden-shafted golf club is shown laid over a reporters steno pad, with both of these lying in a dark bunker on a green course. (This art work only appears on the British printing, and not on the Little Brown or later Grosset & Dunlap editions). This book is chatty, fun, and a fast read.

Here's a quick-fire, wise-cracking mystery story from America. Larry Ray, due to retire from news reporting, decided it was time to publish the diary he had kept for many years. This diary was chiefly a record of the activities of the great; many of them the kind of "activities" it does not pay to advertise. There were in fact quite a number of people in New York City prepared to go to almost any lengths to keep that diary from getting into print ,even to the length of murder! The tale of these lethal memoirs is told by Jack Jordon, ace reporter and amateur sleuth, with speed, humor and plenty of action.

Golf comes into the story late in the book but it is critical to the third murder and to the solution of the other two. From this story we also add to the list of bizarre murder methods involving golf. The way golf is used in this story is truly weird, but still somewhat probable.

***Duke, Will*, William Campbell Gault, US, 1910 - 1996**
Other pseudonyms: *Dial Forest, Roney Scott*
FAIR PREY

Graphic Publishing, New Jersey, 1956, Paperback original

T. V. Boardman, London 1958, 188 pages, 19cm

This is the only known work by the prolific William Gault as Will Duke and only known golf mystery under any of his pseudonyms. However, in addition to full length mysteries, he wrote numerous mystery short stories and, juvenile sports books. It's very possible there is a golf book among them.

At thirteen Denny Burke won the Southern California Junior Championship. He was a regular caddie at Canyon Country Club and encouraged by the pro to play as often as work and school allowed. At sixteen he shot a 64 from the championship tees and made the local papers. He was long off the tee, a decent putter, and his only weakness (if someone who shoots 64 has one) was his middle irons. He captained the college golf team and picked up school expense money playing high rolling members at Canyon CC. The members granted him full membership privileges during his college days.

Taking a job in the pro shop after graduation allowed Denny to continue free play and, time to decide about the pro tour. However, things were very different as an employee! He was severely embarrassed by a drunken member in front of others he regularly played with, and, the wealthiest member of the club wasn't pleased that his daughter, Judy, was serious about Denny. To top it off, during a round of golf, Denny and Judy find the loud mouthed member in the rough, murdered! The police detective thinks Denny is a pretty good suspect.

If there was a ten best list, this one would be on it!. There is golf on nearly every page. Preparation, practice, and competition are knowledgeably described as are the sacrifices required to play at the professional level–and win. The US paperback original can still be found in the used book racks, but the British hardcover is much more difficult to acquire.

Dunnett, Dorothy, née Dorothy Halliday, Scotland , 1923

MATCH FOR A MURDERER

Houghton Mifflin, New York, 1971, 306 pages, 21.5 cm

DOLLY AND THE DOCTOR BIRD

Cassell, London, 1971,

Another British edition, same title, was issued under the author's birth name, Halliday.

Written by a master storyteller, this book is one of a series organized around Johnson Johnson and his boat Dolly. In each book, Johnson, a sailor and respected portrait painter, who is really a spy, gets involved with a capable, resourceful, and indeed, winsome woman. In this book, there is also gorgeous weather and good golf.

Doctor Beltanno Douglas MacRannoch is a no-nonsense, thirty-two year old, Edinburgh-educated physician who obtains an appointment to a Nassau hospital. This post enables her to keep a close eye on her ailing father, the clan chief of Clan MacRannoch, who has relocated from Scotland to the Caribbean. A single woman, the doctor is able to play golf almost every day, and she is good. She is also good with guns, having learned on the best grouse moors in Scotland.

Johnson has come to Nassau to find out who has poisoned a British secret agent. The pretty doctor happens to have been a witness. Any number of quirky suspects are on hand, because the clan chief is holding a worldwide gathering of the clan, including its one Japanese member.

There is a second poisoning, which fails, a shooting that does not fail, an American agent who is (accidentally?) set on fire in a bar, and a lady murdered and thrown into a deep fairway hazard.

The principal suspects are narrowed down to four. Among other things, they all desire to marry the doctor (and become clan chief?), and they all play golf. A golf match is arranged, to smoke out the killer and to decide, with the doctor's consent, who will become her husband.

Durbridge, Francis, British, 1912 -
A GAME OF MURDER
Hodder & Stoughton, London, 1975, 192 pages, 19 cm

This is an interesting read, with some witty dialog and, clever twists. The only golf is a very long slice and its tragic consequences. The sex and violence are sanitized and very mild by American standards.

How far can you hit a slice? A real bad slice, one that will cross completely over the adjoining fairway? Is it possible to slice a ball 225 yards in the air, with enough force at its end to strike a man in the head and knock him unconscious?

Harry Dawson doesn't think so. His dad, Tom Dawson, had gone to his golf club that morning to practice some short shots, after which Harry was to meet him at the clubhouse for lunch. When Harry gets to the club, instead of lunch, he finds his dad dead.

The story is that Tom, practicing short shots from behind a green, was struck in the head with a sliced drive from a tee a full 225 yards away. Stunned, Tom had fallen backwards into a creek, striking his head on a boulder in the creek bed. This second blow killed him.

Harry arrives in time to watch medics load his father's body into an ambulance and take him to the morgue. An extremely shaken man named Newton introduces himself and admits to hitting the drive and seeing it hit Tom.

Harry studies the scene like the trained police investigator he is. There is no golf ball in sight! Where is it? Returning to the apartment which father and son shared, Harry finds an envelope with an auto license number on it, and learns it matches Newton's car. Harry phones Newton, and they agree to a meeting at Newton's home that night. When there is no answer at Newton's upstairs apartment, Harry goes back to his car and finds Newton's body stuffed into the front seat! A killer with a sense of humor. There are a couple more murders, all in the cozy style.

Elkins, Charlotte & Aaron, US

A WICKED SLICE

St. Martins Press, New York, 1989, 198 pages, 21 cm

Charlotte has joined forces with her already very successful mystery writer husband, and they produce a dandy the first time out. This is the first of hopefully a long series. The golf is knowingly described, as are the pressures of being an unsponsored and as yet unsuccessful tour player. This is wonderful stuff.

As her first year on the Ladies' Professional Golf Tour ends, Lee Ofsted has all the problems of the typical tour rookie, a.k.a., *rabbit*. She hasn't won a tournament— in fact she hasn't won enough so far to avoid losing her pro card. If that happens, she will have to return to the qualifying school and start all over.

She's almost out of what little expense money she had and now she has developed a terrible slice with her three wood. Only with her three wood! She is two days into a new tournament when she finally figures out that the club has been altered. Hitting balls from the far right end of the practice range, she watches one of her slices go into the nearby pond and splash. Beside a floating body? Running down there, she pulls to shore the body of the tour's leading money winner.

There is some immediate chemistry between Lee and the handsome police detective lieutenant who is assigned the case. He knows nothing about golf or the tour and Lee agrees to fill him in, over dinner. He likes that but he is very upset about one of Lee's Pro-Am partners. Peg is a very high-powered business woman, accustomed to getting her way, and she decides to assist in the murder investigation. It turns out that she has some helpful connections. Another murder, a very quirky caddie, and four rounds of extremely competitive women's professional golf make this a keeper.

ROTTEN LIES

Mysterious Press, New York, 1995, 230 pages, 23.5 cm

Lee's quirky caddie, her detective boyfriend, and Pushy Peggy are all back in this one. There's some exciting golf, with gut knotting scrambling shots, and go-for-it drives over hazards. Buy it and enjoy it!

Lee Ofsted is still struggling. Last year she won all of eleven thousand dollars. But her game is getting better and better. In the opening round, the Pro-Am of the High Desert Classic, she shot a life time score. Her 64 was not only her best ever, it's a new course record for Cottonwood Creek Country Club and she is the tournament leader after one round. Lighting has finally struck!

Actually, it strikes a number of times. It stops play the second day. When it does, Lee takes cover, waits for a break in the storm, and then heads back to the club house. On the way, she discovers the burned body of the president of Cottonwood Creek, lying in the rough.

In a futile effort to revive him, she twists her left elbow and takes herself out of the tournament and off the tour for at least six weeks. She gets a career saving break when the tournament TV producer uses her for color commentary and likes her style. Then the police announce that the president's death wasn't an accident. How do you kill someone with lightning?

The next day, Lee's friendly TV producer is poisoned at breakfast in front of the whole tournament committee and TV crew.

Lee's friend Peg is a member of the committee and she again involves herself in the murder investigations. There's a lot about the televising of a golf tournament and some about the current practice of converting classic old golf courses into new golf resorts. The money is welcome but the classic course is destroyed with design gimmicks that infuriate the old time purists.

Ellroy, James, US, 1948 -
BROWN'S REQUIEM

Avon, New York, 1981, Paperback original, 256 pages

Allison & Busby, London, 1984, 256 pages,

Brown's Requiem was the author's first published work. He continues to produce and, is very popular and, collectible. His stories have a jagged hard edge, which may be reflective of his life on the streets following the murder of his mother when he was a young teen. He is self-educated and a unique piece of work. He loves music and at times performs with a band.

This book has a lot about the lifestyle of professional country club caddies, who are not college kids earning summer money. These are drunks, habitual gamblers, and every other kind of social misfit. In spite of all this, they love the game of golf, and appreciate the opportunity to caddie for good players. A very different look at the game.

Fritz Brown is asked to resign from the Los Angeles Police Department. His drinking problem and abusive treatment of people have embarrassed his superiors, and he has no redeeming features with which to mitigate their low opinion of him.

Brown finds work as a repo man, taking back cars from owners who are behind in their payments. He is unconcerned that the car dealer he works for makes a practice of selling cars with such high payment schedules that default is a forgone conclusion. The repo work pays well and keeps him in classical music records.

Freddy "Fat Dog" Baker seeks Brown out and asks him to investigate the man whom Freddy's sister is living with. Freddy is loaded! He carries a roll of hundred dollar bills that have to be jammed into the pocket of his worn-out golf slacks. Freddy works as a caddie at the more prestigious country clubs in the Los Angeles area. Because he fears being inside, he sleeps outside, on the golf course.

With a substantial retainer in hand, Brown starts digging. Pornography, arson, murder, and incest are mixed with classical music under the stars at the Hollywood Bowl and a week drunk in Mexico.

The US paperback original can still be found in the used book store racks, but the British hardcover is difficult.

Engleman, Paul, US, 1953 -
MURDER IN-LAW

Mysterious Press, New York, 1987, 248 pages, 21.5 cm

Golf, sex, drugs, and murders keep this story supercharged!

Dwight Robinson had been hailed as the Black Mickey Mantle. Life was good when he made the Yankees and married his school sweetheart. Then it all comes apart. Busted for drugs, he is suspended from the game by the baseball commissioner.

It gets much worse. He comes home to find Cynthia, his twenty-one year old wife, dead on the living room floor. He calls the police and they arrest him for murder. His father-in-law screams for his conviction. It does not help that the father-in-law, Thomas Vreeland, is very rich, politically connected, and white.

Private detective Mark Renzler is also a former big league ball player. His career was ruined by a beanball that cost him an eye. He takes Robinson's case and heads for Mountain Lake, New Jersey, to investigate.

A very private community, Mountain Lake was built from scratch by Thomas Vreeland, for the well-to-do who love golf. Enormous homes surround the golf course and social life revolves around the clubhouse. The winding drive up to Vreeland's own front door is flanked by life-size statues of Snead, Hogan, Nicklaus, and others.

Renzler is thrown out of Vreeland's home, but not before meeting Terry and Tommy Vreeland, Cynthia's siblings. Terry, scratch golfer and beautiful, does not believe Dwight killed her sister.

Terry and Mark team up, and the investigation reveals Tommy's drug deals. It also reveals that Daddy was buying up properties in the flood plain, for next to nothing, with insider knowledge of a highway project to come. The investigation coincides with preparation for the Annual Mountain Lake Celebrity Golf Outing.

All the principals in the murders (there have been a couple more) are involved in the tournament, so Renzler decides to solve the case on the course. There is some very good golf played by Terry, who is leaving for the LPGA qualifying school soon. There is also some terrible golf played by luminaries who only get out for these events.

Fairlie, Gerard, British, 1899 - 1983

Bernard Darwin, The top golf writer, is quoted on the back panel of the dust jacket, saying, "Mr. Fairlie has added new terror to golf." Fairlie was Darwin's assistant at *The Times of London* for two years and went on to be the golf correspondent at *The Bystander* for five years. In this story, the plot is not very deep by today's standards, but it is still an interesting read

MR. MALCOLM PRESENTS

Hodder & Stoughton, London, 1932, 314 pages, 19 cm

The story takes place in St. Andrews, Scotland, as the British Amateur is being played over the Old Course. Bobby Jones is challenging Cyril Tolley, current champion, for the title and the whole of Britain is following the matches.

All Dundee, which was enjoying its half-holiday, seemed to have come to the classic course. All Edinburgh seemed to have joined forces. A narrow pathway from tee to green, true, had been kept by the stewards waving their little red flags, but everywhere else, apparently, the black spots were swarming. Dundee and Edinburgh were in force. And–in this lay the comforting thought to the bad guy–not only were Dundee and Edinburgh in force upon the golf course, but also all St. Andrews, man, woman, and child.

The bad guy has just committed murder, and he is counting on the attention of everyone being on the match and allowing him to carry off his crime undetected.

Mr. Malcolm, like his creator, is also an avid golf fan, although not much of a player. He is generally satisfied with a single good shot each round and prefers that it come in the last few holes so it is fresh in his memory when the game is over. Mr. Malcolm has an undefined relationship with the police based on his ability to solve mysteries.

Here he offers his crime-solving services to the hotel in which a murder has taken place. When the hotel manager comes to regret this arrangement, Mr. Malcolm goes to work with the police. None of this is laid out in specific terms, but, is understood.

In the final pages, Mr. Malcolm confronts the killer and is forced to play an unusual golf match with him. The stakes are life and death for the killer, a beautiful young lady being held hostage, and Mr. Malcolm. The description of the match between Jones and Tolley sparkles..

SHOT IN THE DARK

Hodder & Stoughton, London, 1932, 315 pages, 19 cm
Doubleday, New York, 1932,

There is not much golf in this story but, like the typical hacker, it is done with enthusiasm and immense pleasure when a shot comes off. Questioned once about a just-completed round, Mr. Malcolm says, *"We must have a drink to celebrate, it's not often that I drive well. I insist, most emphatically. It's not everyday that I carry the bunker at the third hole from the tee!"* A hard book to find but worth the effort.

Peter Browne is old, haggard, worn with illness, ugly with ill-temper, very wealthy, and convinced someone is going to kill him. He is right—he is murdered in his bed. Death is caused by a gunshot to the head, so there is an inquest.

The Coroner is able to convince the jurors that death was caused by the deceased. The verdict is suicide—very determined suicide, because the evidence shows that two shots were fired with the first shot missing completely.

The local police authority enlist Mr. Malcolm to conduct an unofficial investigation. This is not a unique request, as Mr. Malcolm has an undefined relationship with the police based on his facility as a solver of mysteries.

Mr. Malcolm, an avid, though poor golfer, starts his investigation by deliberately hitting a drive through the library window (remarkable shot), where Browne's family has gathered to hear the will.

Mr. Malcolm retrieves his ball and inserts himself into the gathering, who have just heard the deceased accuse one of them, via a recording, of murder. The family reluctantly agrees that Mr. Malcolm should determine if it was murder and, if so, find the killer. Within a short time, Mr. Malcolm obtains three confessions; two which claim to have fired the fatal shot and one claiming to have poisoned Mr. Browne.

Mr. Malcolm sets up a quick round of golf with his primary suspect on the course next to the house, and ends up left for dead in a storage building when rain disrupts the match.

MEN FOR COUNTERS

Hodder and Stoughton, London, 1933, 313 pages, 18 cm

Men For Counters is a 1933 version of a contemporary international thriller. There is not much golf here, but the golf takes place in adventures in the Brazilian jungle. This is the only golf mystery series we know of that Bernard Dawin allowed his name to be used in the promotion of. He and the author apparently enjoyed a professional understanding founded in their love of the game of golf.

Alex Grame, Scotsman, and Tony Valais of France have been in Brazil for four years. Their respective governments lent them to the Brazilian government to gather evidence against Don Jose Alvares, the richest man in Brazil. Alvares controls all the engineering and construction businesses in the country. People have been dying because his projects fall apart.

After three years of having witnesses disappear or change their testimony, Grame and Valais finally obtain the evidence and try to get it out of the country. Alvares' men capture them in the jungle and take them to his secret estate, on which he has constructed a golf course. The course, one fairway with greens and tees at each end, is as lovely as any in Scotland.

Grame, a scratch player three years ago, is pressed into a game with his captor. Grame wins and, during a second game the next day, he plays a fantastic shot which enables the pair to escape. Back in England they learn their latest evidence is worthless, as Alvares has gotten to their witness.

Mr. Malcolm makes his entrance half way through the book as Grame's playing partner on his first day back in Scotland. Mr. Malcolm has been assigned, by the British government, to protect Grame.om Alvares, seeking revenge, has followed him to England. Alvares has brought beautiful bait with him and Grame, his hormones out of control, is captured again. Mr. Malcolm to the rescue!

Ferrars, Elizabeth*, British, 1907 -, Pseudonym of Morna Doris MacTaggart Brown, US Byline: *E.X. Ferrars
THE SEVEN SLEEPERS
William Collins, London, 1970,
Doubleday, New York, 1970, 222 pages,

There is very little golf played in this story, but the locality, near the gates to golf heaven on earth, will satisfy most readers. The story is gripping and soon consumed.

On a foggy Sunday morning in Blackhope, East Lothian, Scotland, a little old lady is murdered. She has just moved from Edinburgh to a newly redecorated cottage, next door to her brother and his wife. Her Edinburgh apartment was up two flights of steep stairs, and her family insisted that all the going up and down was not doing her bad heart any good. She moved to the cottage for her health, but before she completed the unpacking, she is killed.

Her cottage looks out over a seaside golf course. On a clear day, one can see beyond, across the Firth of Forth to Fifeshire. It is but a short way, then, to St. Andrews.

Of course, most people here golf. The course and the water are wonderful to look at, and it is so convenient to walk out the door-wall and onto the course. The down side is the terrific explosion and the flying glass caused every time a hooked tee shot shatters the door-wall.

The old lady is found with shattered glass all over her body and a golf ball on the floor near her head. The time of her death, and the time that play on the course was stopped due to heavy fog, turn out to be critical elements in the case. The alibi of each of the suspects is checked against the fog coming in.

A couple of suspects are excellent golfers and fully capable of driving a ball through a target as large as a door-wall. Maybe the killer's goal was not actually to hit the old lady, but rather, to explode the window while she was right next to it, counting on her weak heart doing the rest.

Her whole family was extremely upset with her because lately she insisted on digging into an old family scandal.

Fleming, Ian, British, 1908 - 1964

GOLDFINGER

Jonathan Cape, London, 1959, 318 pages, 19.5 cm

Macmillan, New York, 1959, 318 pages, 19.5 cm

007! James Bond, the British Secret Service agent licensed to kill, is the main character. He dashes around the world, dressed—when he is dressed—in evening clothes, beautiful women on his arm. Like all 007 books, this one has fast cars, tricky gadgets for killing the enemy, and always the beautiful women. But it also has some of the best golf depicted in the whole of golf mysteries. Don't miss this one.

In this assignment, Bond is to get the goods on Goldfinger, who is smuggling gold out of England at a rate that threatens the British banking system. Bond must find out how it is being done and stop it.

Early in the story, Bond is able to arrange a golf match with Goldfinger, who loves to gamble at cards and especially at golf. Then for thirty-two pages the reader is exposed to some of the best match play golf ever written. Ian Fleming obviously knows something about great golf writing, as he quotes from a Bernard Darwin article.

The match, which takes place on Royal St. Marks at Sandwich, features match play with just the two players and their caddies. The play is even, as both admit to playing off a nine handicap. There are great shots, poor shots, and, then there is cheating. The conditions laid down at the start were to play by the strict rules of golf. Hardly!

The Fleming collectors have run up the price of this book, and the first editions are difficult to find. (There's a surprise under the dust jacket. The front cover has a skull embossed in it, with gold coins in the eye holes.)

This book has been reprinted in hardcover by book clubs and also in paperback. This story was a very successful movie and it is available on video. The golf sequence is shorter in the movie, but wonderful! Goldfinger's caddie, Odd Job, is a classic.

Fletcher, J(oseph) S(mith), British, 1863 - 1935
THE PERILOUS CROSSWAYS
Ward, Lock & Company, London, 1917, 312 pages
Hillman, New York, 1938,

The title and the plot revolve around a golf course with a chalk pit in the middle of it. The plot is very involved, with several false leads and double-backs. This is one of the most difficult titles to locate–the author of **The Golf Murders** finally settled for reading it in The Library of Congress. Look hard, but count yourself lucky if you find a copy.

James Muary has been back in England for only one day, after many years in India, when he is murdered. Upon first returning, he is met in London by his nephew, Herbert Muary. At lunch in the city, Herbert apprises his uncle of his thwarted plans to marry Miss Madeya Erringham. Miss Madeya, the daughter of Colonel Erringham, is engaged to Alan Rysedale.

James Muary is incensed at this news. He knows Marcius Rysedale, Alan's father, and regards him as a rogue of the lowest order. He feels obliged to inform his old friend, the Colonel, of the kind of family his daughter is about to marry into.

When James and his nephew arrive at the Muary family estate, which James owns, he announces that he will walk over to Erringham's in the morning and have a talk with the Colonel.

The Muary and Erringham estates are separated by a very nice golf course. To facilitate visiting, the fences have gates and a pathway crosses the course. The pathway leads into an old chalk pit located in the center of the fifth fairway. The pit makes the fifth the most difficult hole on the course, as it has to be carried. A ball hit into the pit is certain to be unplayable.

Miss Madeya is on the course early the next morning. She is to play with Alan, but declines to wait for him and starts alone. Despite her resolve to conquer the fifth, she watches her drive fall into the tangle at the bottom of the pit.

She enlists young Tommy Cole, who happens by, to help her find the ball. Instead they find James Muary, stabbed in the heart and quite dead. Found near the body is a fresh handkerchief embroidered with the initials M.R.

Flynn, J. M., US, 1927 - 1985
TERROR TOURNAMENT
Thomas Bouregy & Co., NY, 1959, 220 pages, 20 cm

The only golf played in this story is a loopy swing with a long iron to the main character's head. There is a lot about how to, or, how not-to, provide security for a major golf event.

Burl Stannard considered himself to be a pretty good cop. But he does not like rules and restrictions, and his chief did not like his attitude. After Burl lost his temper during an attitude adjustment speech by the chief, he took his badge and threw it on the desk.

Not knowing much else, Burl has gone into the security business. His first job is to protect the gate receipts of a local pro-am golf tournament. When the tournament is being held on one of the famous courses on the Monterey peninsula, and the amateurs are big-name celebrities, the gate receipts are considerable.

Burl's job is to guard the tournament, count the gate receipts, and then take the four hundred thousand dollars to the bank. Before the bank-limo gets to the main gate, a gang of hoods in golf carts surround it, kill the driver, take the money, and escape in their carts.

When Burl, who was knocked unconscious during the hold-up, comes to, he goes to the pro shop to check cart rental records. Inside the pro shop, he is laid out again, this time with a long iron to the back of the head. Having lost the gate receipts and the cart rental records, and having been knocked out twice, he changes tactics and goes to the bar with his beautiful secretary. Later, following up on another suspect, Burl finds another body on the course.

***Frome, David*, Zenith Jones Brown, US, 1898-1983**

Other Pseudonyms: *Leslie Ford, Brenda Conrad*

THE STRANGE DEATH OF MARTIN GREEN

Doubleday Crime Club, NY, 1931, 309 pages, 19.5 cm

THE MURDER ON THE SIXTH HOLE

Methuen, London, 1931, 216 pages, 19.5 cm

The golf's good. The ending is very tricky.

South Forest Country Club, with its green velvet golf course and crystal sparkling river, is electric with tensions. Fueled by virulent anti-Semitism and coarse racism, the atmosphere fairly crackles. No one is surprised when Martin Green, the Jewish developer who created South Forest, and its most hated member, is found dead on the course.

Very early on a Sunday morning, a twosome walks up the hill to the sixth tee. A golf bag is on the ground, and a tee peg is placed very near the edge of the sharp drop-off. The two players surmise the bag belongs to Green, who is probably looking for a lost ball. He carries only two balls, and will not pay the caddies to look for his errant shots.

The two players do not want to join with Green, and decide to walk ahead to the seventh tee, skipping the sixth. First, they take a look over the edge and see a ball, stuck in the grass a few feet below. Then they see the body! It is lying face down in the pond. They can tell from the tee that it is Green and that he is dead.

The sixth is the most difficult hole. The pond, actually a swamp, fills the entire ninety yards between the tee and the sixth green. The river is right behind the green. Any shot over the green goes into the river. Anything short finishes in the swamp, from which there is no possible shot.

An English house guest of a prominent member had played with Green the day before. At the sixth, Green had asked for and gotten advice on playing the hole. Immediately following the discovery of Green's body, his partner of the previous day examines the sixth tee. From the location of Green's tee peg, he determines that this was no accident, that Green was literally thrown to his death.

Fuller, Timothy
REUNION WITH MURDER
Atlantic Little Brown, Boston, 1941, 258 pages, 19.5 cm
Heinemann, London, 1947, 153 pages, 19 cm

Harvard, class of '31, has gathered for their tenth year anniversary. The three day reunion starts at Syonsett Resort, a couple of hours drive from Cambridge where it will end with a rally in the stadium. For most, this is the first time together since graduation and there's much to catch up on. It's done in the bar, over cards, tennis, the beach and golf. The first foursome on the course the morning of the second day discovers a body on the eleventh tee. The dead man, lying on his back with his arms at his sides and dressed in his dinner jacket, is positioned exactly between the tee markers. The scene resembles an ancient sacrificial ritual with the victim on the altar waiting the knife. Only, this man, Sherman North, Harvard '31, investment banker, has been shot through the heart. North's car is nearby, wiped clean of fingerprints. There's also a trail of footprints, made by a woman's high heel shoes, leading from the hotel parking lot, across the fairway and ending on the tee next to the body.

Ed Rice, North's designated roommate, was awakened with a pounding hangover. He could not explain North's unused bed, the bloody abrasions on his right hand or the blood spots on his dinner shirt of last evening. Rice (being Harvard '31) knew these things looked suspicious. He immediately phoned Harvard Literature Professor, Juniper Jones, former classmate, whose avocation is crime detection. Juniper, scheduled to be married tomorrow, goes to Syonett to solve the murder, and clear Rice, his best man. One plot element involves the alibi of two men, last seen with North, which consisted of their playing golf by moonlight until they lost most of their balls.. The book is replete with social, political, and economic commentary of the time. There's little actual golf played but it's central to the story.

Furlong, Nicola, Canada,
TEED OFF

Commonwealth Publications, Edmonton, 1996, 399 pages, Paperback original

There are not many professional golfers from Canada, men or women. The playing season is just too short to enable a young golfer to get good. But the Quinn sisters made it. Halliday, the oldest has twenty-nine wins and one more puts her in the LPGA Hall of Fame. Riley came out on the tour a few years ago and won twice before the accident that ended her pro career. She went back to Western Canada and a head pro job at Sea Blush, a shiny new course built by Halliday's estranged husband, Peter "Pitts" Windamere.

Pitts is a high flying land developer and he means to kick off Sea Blush in style. He lands a LPGA tour event and everyone is breaking there butts to get things ready for the women pro golfers.

Riley had extracted a promise from Pitts to not drink alone, the reason his marriage is wrecked. She was the one who found him, dead from a fall from his condo deck to the woods below. She was doubly sick when the coroner's report came back, showing a very high level of alcohol.

The police and the coroner were leaning toward accidental death, maybe even suicide because of the drugs that were also found by the autopsy. Riley can't buy it! She knew that Pitts had enemies and that he had received threatening letters from radical environmentalists about the new course. She would not let it rest.

The tournament starts and Riley is caddying for sister Halliday. Both decided that Pitts would want them in it rather than withdrawing. Riley's accident, in a car driven by Halliday, is never discussed but always present.

There's enough emotional stuff going on in this one to keep a person in analysis for life. There is also a whole lot of very good, high level, competition golf. Riley even gets in the pro-am and despite the pain of her old injury, finishes her team in the money.

Gibbins, James
SUDDEN DEATH
Collins Crime Club, London, 1983, 210 pages, 20 cm

Published only in England and fairly common in the used book shops there, this book is difficult to find in the US. The dust jacket is one of our favorites, featuring a hand grenade and golf club.

There are a couple of other golf mysteries by the same or similar titles as this one, so double check your collector's lists when ordering from catalogs.

Winston Churchill is quoted in this book as saying "Golf is the game of the Devil'. That would have made an excellent title for this book, given its sinister and twisted plot.

This story has lots of competitive golf, played in a mine field! The plot is so strange that you are sure to finish the book, if only to see who is left after a series of explosions.

A terminally ill, very rich man, is taking revenge against his treacherous son by changing the provisions of his will. He decides to award his total fortune, $250 million, to the winner of an invitation-only golf tournament. The players are all scratch or better and on the run from the law: terrorists, Mafia fugitives, con men, and so forth.

The players are all men who the sponsor believes are primarily motivated by greed. They will need to be, because the golf course, specially built in Southeast Asia just for this tournament, is mined! Players who trip a mine will be blown up. A special ground crew fills in the craters and plants new mines so that play can go on, almost uninterrupted. And there is a newly constructed hospital alongside the course to serve those players who trip a mine and are not killed outright.

There is no hero in this story, or even a nice person, except possibly the Eurasian hooker who falls for the former golf pro from the States. He had left the tour, via a drug habit that had destroyed his game and taken all his winnings. He did a prison stretch for attempted bank robbery, trying to get money for dope.

***Gray, Jonathan*, British, 1874 - 1958, Pseudonym of Herbert Adams**

THE OWL

Harrap, London, 1937, 272 pages, 18.5 cm

Lippincott, Philadelphia, 1937, 272 pages,

This book, which may be Adams' best, is sadly very scarce. There is a lot of golf- the lifestyle of the story's high society young people is to play golf and tennis during the day and party every night.

A daring jewel thief is driving Scotland Yard crazy. He has pulled off a number of spectacular jobs, which are covered exhaustively by the papers. As though to taunt the police, the jewel thief leaves a card behind, containing a small drawing of an owl. Then, a few days after each job, he sends a small cash donation to the police widows' fund.

While looking foolish, the police know it would be even worse if the press and, public, knew what the police suspect. It seems that the Owl may be one of a small group of men who regularly play golf together. There are five in the group, and one of them is a Scotland Yard Inspector assigned to the Owl's case. It may even be that two or more of the group are working together to commit these crimes.

A couple of times, all five have been invited guests at a home which immediately after became the site of an Owl jewel heist. Their golf matches keep them talking, even as the tension of being suspects strains their friendship.

Matters are complicated by a trio of romances among the players. One elopes with the bride-to-be of a man recently the victim of the Owl. The victim has now lost his bride and, his jewels, possibly to the same man. The tormented victim is further infuriated when his daughter takes up with another of the five.

A third member of the five is falling for the female reporter assigned by her newspaper to unmask the Owl. These last two duel on and off the golf course.

Gregson, J. M., British,

This series was a wonderful discovery. The writing is tight and full of British understatement and wit. The golf is brilliantly depicted from a lifetime's experience of playing, with an awareness of the mixed pain and pleasure of this great game. Gregson describes his own golf as playing off an arthritic 5 at age 61.

Featuring Superintendent Lambert, a golfing man, and his assistant Sergeant Hook, who thinks golf a silly sport at best, the series is now up to nine titles. Only two qualify so far as golf mysteries and are featured here. The author has advised that the tenth, called **Body Politic**, will introduce Hook, screaming all the way, to golf!

MURDER AT THE NINETEENTH

Collins Crime Club, London, 1989, 206 pages, 22 cm

While there is not a lot of golf played in this sparkling mystery, the day-to-day operation of a golf club is covered in interesting detail. Both Lambert and the club's Lady Captain, a murder suspect, are flower garden hobbyists, and the golf course flora is also described in interesting detail.

The Chairman of a local golf club is murdered in the club house committee room following a meeting. All committee members who attended are suspects. The investigation is supervised by Police Superintendent John Lambert, a club member and Chairman of the Green's committee.

Lambert is a twenty-five-year police veteran and quite professional, but very uncomfortable interrogating his friends as possible murderers. To break the ice, he tries one interview on the course but its unsuccessful. It soon turns out that the victim, a successful businessman, is universally disliked. Everyone at the meeting had a motive to kill him.

As the investigation gathers facts, the murderer panics and kills again. The first killing was managed with a single stab of a large knife. This second requires multiple blows with a five iron. It appears the pressure may be putting the killer off his game?

DEAD ON COURSE

Collins Crime Club, London, 1991, 189 pages, 22 cm

Another good one from this author. There is not a lot of golf, but it is fondly described. About the location, the dust jacket says, *"The golf course and hotel are set in spectacular scenery beside one of England's most beautiful rivers, with the square tower of Hereford's ancient Cathedral visible in the distance."*

In this second golf mystery, Superintendent Lambert and Sergeant Hook, investigate a murder committed on a golf course. Lambert plays off a single-digit handicap and enjoys a game whenever he can get one. Here he plays with the three principal murder suspects and rationalizes it as a way to watch them up close. Sergeant Hook, his subordinate, *and do not ever forget it*, regards this as a serious digression from standard police investigative procedure.

The first victim appears to have been pushed to his death from the hotel rooftop, on which his golfing group and assorted ladies had gathered to enjoy the evening sky and sip a little wine after dinner. But the body is discovered out on the course the next morning and preliminary evidence suggests that the person who moved it was not the killer.

Digging deeper, the police find that everyone, including the victim's wife, is happy to have him dead. So, if he was unanimously disliked, even hated, why was he invited to be the fourth golfer on a week-long golf vacation? Another murder involves equally confusing circumstances.

Greig, Ian, British

THE KING'S CLUB MURDER

Ernest Benn Limited, London, 1930, 288 pages, 19 cm

THE SILVER KING MYSTERY

Henry Holt, New York, 1930, 288 pages,

The British version is far more common but the dust jacket of either printing is rare. The author used golf, although less of it, in **Murder At Lintercombe** (*these failed to* *make the cut* section) which it is worth the hunt. The author is credited with three other mysteries (not seen) and it is quite possible there will be golf in one or more of them.

Amelia Piltar, a peculiar old lady, lives in a large house that abuts the grounds of the King's Club golf club. For her own purposes, she secretly had a gate made in the hedge at the back of her garden so she can walk onto the course.

Inspector Swinton, a newly promoted inspector , receives the assignment to investigate her murder. He happens to be the only investigator on duty and not busy with other cases. The other, more expierenced investigators might have been less than eager to take the King's Club case, because they know it is the personal club of the Chief Inspector, who expects the investigator to show up promply, investigate quickly, and make an arrest before lunch.

Swinton finds the victim, Miss Piltar, lying in the eighteenth fairway, with two marks on the back of her neck. Each mark perfectly matches the mesh pattern of the Silver King golf ball. It turns out that about half the members play the Silver King, including the Chief Inspector. Further investigation determines that she was not killed by the blows to the head, but rather was strangled by the carrying strap of a golf bag.

The victim was last seen practicing chip shots in the fairway next to her home. Playing in the last foursome to pass her, was her nephew, who is also her sole heir. When her home is searched for a possible motive for the killing, it is found that she was a very active blackmailer.

Late in the story, there is a wonderfully exciting car chase, and the introduction of an undetectable (without getting right down to it) female impersonator who is central to the solution. There is also a scene in which a beautiful young lady, whom Swinton had previously met and was dazzled by, is abducted, stripped of all her clothes, and tied spread-eagled to a farm gate. This has the desired effect of slowing Swinton down in his pursuit of the killer. Swinton is the perfect gentleman and preserves the lady's dignity and the cozy classification of the book.

Hamer, Malcolm, British

The author has worked in the field of sports management and represented a number of top sportsmen. His experiences have provided him with the inside material to produce this quite different golf mystery series. It is told from the other side of the bag. The protagonist, Chris Ludlow, is a pro tour caddie, but not just any caddie. He's had an expensive university education (paid for by his parents) and he knows first hand that an impressive amateur golf record is not necessarily transferable to a career on the pro tour.

SUDDEN DEATH

Headline Books, London, 1991, 344 pages, 24 cm

There are not enough events on the British golf tour, even if he had a bag to carry in all them, to keep Chris in the style he's accustomed to. Tapping into the *old-boy-network*, he lands a position as a stockbroker in London. The firm's owner is golf crazy. He's delighted to have an employee who can help him with his game, dazzle the firm's customers on the golf course and introduce him to the pro's. Chris quickly displays an aptitude for uncovering new companies, especially in the entertainment field, that have a better than average prospect for stock appreciation. The salary is good, his father is pleased, and he gets time off to caddie some tour events. He achieves a degree of celebrity when the press dubs him 'the upper crust caddie'.

Chris has a new bag. He's carrying for Jack Mason, one of the best. But no one is winning in England this year except Brian Harley, whose career was supposed to be over due to years of booze. Now, Harley is the hottest thing on tour because he can't miss a putt. He's making everything and Chris is a little suspicious. Walking the fairways one morning to get yardages for his golfer, Chris finds the body of a murdered tour caddie - Harley's caddie - and he's got a putter shaft stuck through his neck. A second caddie is murdered and Chris teams up with a newspaper golf writer to investigate. To speed up the process the writer suggests in his column that he and Chris are onto the facts behind the killings. That results in both of them getting savage beatings.

There's plenty of golf, both on tour and the equally serious games played between salesmen and customers. Along with the murders and, detecting, there's discussions of the working of the stock markets and insider trading. The manufacture and marketing of golf equipment, especially putters, and the interesting issue of player endorsements is neatly worked into the plot. In addition to a good mystery, here's an inside peek at golf as an industry.

A DEADLY LIE

Headline Books, London, 1992, 310 pages, 24 cm

This is a intensely busy time for Chris. His tour pro, Jack Mason, has decided to change caddies, and by way of compensation, introduces Chris to Rollo Hardinge, a young pro with tremendous golfing talent and an indifferent attitude toward the game. With some ambivalence, Chris takes on Rollo's bag. At the same time, his stock brokerage firm is bringing to market a major new public offering. Chris is a main player, due to the stock issue involving a television production firm, a recording business and syndication rights in the US of some hot British programming. The market's soft and there's concern that nothing happen to scare flighty buyers. That's when the female lead of the new TV series, critical to the whole deal, falls to her death from her apartment window. Chris, a family friend, is first on the scene. The police call it suicide.

Much of the golf is centered around Pro-Am's. Many of the celebrities involved in the companies which make up the stock offering, are frequent Pro-Am players. There's even a hotly contested, annual award for the celebrity Pro-Am player with the most Pro-Am points. All kinds of gamesmanship are used by these players as they jockey for the award. Then another member of the TV company dies and there's no doubt this time that it's murder. Becoming exasperated by Rollo's lack of focus, Chris shakes him up, literally. As in **Sudden Death**, there's much going on in this enjoyable book. The golf is terrific and at the same time the financial workings of the entertainment industry are worked in without a ripple.

DEATH TRAP

Headline Books, London, 1993, 246 pages, 24 cm

There's a world wide recession and Chris Ludlow, stock-broker, is one of its casualties. For a while, at least, Chris has to make it financially on the golf course as a tour caddie. It gets worse, when his tour player, whose game is in a slump, goes off to the States to play, with a new caddie to boot! Chris takes no comfort when his former pro quickly records a US tour victory.

When he intervenes in a knife fight in the parking lot of a tour event, Chris finds the fighters to be stepbrothers. One's a tour player of considerable talent. He's also carrying tons of personal baggage, making it impossible to compete at a world class level, with any prospect of winning. He secures Chris as combination caddie/counselor. In very short order the bad step brother is shot dead and Chris's pro disappears. Trying to clear his pro, Chris's investigation uncovers family secrets involving the pro's real father.

All the while, the British team selection and, strategy for the Rider Cup Competition is going on. In part, because of Chris's efforts, the young pro is chosen for the team and they are off for the US. It soon becomes obvious, someone is trying to sabotage by whatever means, the British team's chances of winning. Chris carries the golf bag and wards off evil attempts by persons unknown to throw his player off his game. There is a goodly amount of high pressure, world class golf, engagingly described. The P.G.A. gets a close look by Hamer and the way endorsements are handled is examined. Golf course and related property development financing are also seamlessly presented in this fast reading and totally enjoyable book.

SHADOWS ON THE GREEN

Headline Books, London, 1994, 249 pages, 24 cm

Chris Ludlow is out of work again. Ex stockbroker, ex tour caddie, and with no real prospects in sight, he gets a call to play in a high stakes team match with his partner covering all bets. The golf described in this early part of the book just doesn't get much better. One of the people Chris plays in the match is involved in the renovation of a famous old country club and the construction of an adjacent 18 holes. Chris gets a job working for the course architect and is involved in a new aspect of the golf scene.

There is a power struggle involving the owner of the old course, the sponsors of a national pro tournament played there every year, and the club members who seem to have no real power in this contest. The whole thing gets ugly when it's determined that the long-time owner of the club just doesn't have the money to make the changes the sponsor demands.

New money can be had, but, at the cost of giving up control. Applications to the local governments for construction permits for the course work are opposed by local conservationists when an endangered bird species is found to nest on the land being considered. Changes in design by the architect satisfy the local opposition but nothing can placate, The Green Disciples. They are a well financed, highly organized and violently militant group who are opposed to the building of all golf courses, period! Their tactics include; moving survey stakes, destroying construction equipment, and burning construction offices. Chris meets the beautiful but dedicated leader of this group and falls for her. When his boss finds out, he assigns Chris the job of getting the Disciples to back off. No chance! There is a couple more deaths along the way.

Chris also gets an opportunity to caddie for an American pro in 'The Open' at St. Andrews and this sequence is worth the price of the book. Hamer continues to fill his mysteries with interesting looks into other aspectss of golf, as well as the pro tour. Another winner!

DEAD ON LINE

Headline Books, London, 1996, 314 pages, 22 cm

This one has it all! Pro golf events, golf course architecture, and lots of stuff about golf collectibles. Early clubs, balls, and paintings, are bought and sold, faked and forged.

When the members of The Royal Dorset Golf Club decided that their course needed a working over, they hired Chris's boss, Calvin Blair, Golf Architect. Blair laid out the changes and then pretty much left Chris to over-see the work. The whole project would take a couple of years and so Chris had a construction office at the course. He enjoyed the work, liked the old course and, the company of the club secretary. Helen Raven, recently retired police inspector, was one of the very few female club secretaries in England. She was friendly and super efficient. One of her self appointed tasks was to obtain a professional appraisal of the golf artifacts owned by the club. She engaged the best and Chris was able to watch him go over the club's collection of golf paintings, Allan Robertson gutta balls, a Hugh Philip driver, and a treasure trove of miscellaneous items. A few nights later, before Helen could arrange to have the items properly secured, they were stolen. The club was broken into and all the artifacts taken. The Club Steward, who had living quarters in the club house, went to investigate. He was beaten and later died. That same night, two other old golf clubs were also burgled and their golfing treasures stolen. Shortly, a well known Japanese golf antiquities dealer was savagely murdered. Then the home of the authority who Helen had hired to appraise Royal Dorset's collection, was itself broken into and a large collection taken. Chris began to suspect the officious authority. There were vague, but none the less, frequently heard rumors that *The Expert* had been connected with a couple of questionable paintings a few years ago? Unable to investigate full time due to a commitment to caddie a few pro events, he enlists the help of a pretty young photographer. Together they haunt the golf auctions to get the evidence.

Hamilton, Patrick, British, 1904 - 1962

HANGOVER SQUARE or THE MAN WITH TWO MINDS

Constable, London, 1941,

Random House, New York, 1942

This is not an ordinary mystery. The mystery here is whether or not the crime (murder) will ever really happen, and if so, what then?The book opens with a description of schizophrenia. "Schizophrenia; a cleavage of the mental functions, associated with assumption of the affected person of a second personality".

The story is set in London in 1939 and war is imminent. It starts as the story is ending. This is not a fun read but there's a terrific golf sequence in it which could change the final outcome.

George Harvey Bone is schizophrenic. He has two separate personalities which snap back and forth into place, each never knowing what the other is doing. He has had this condition since his school days and thinks that he can handle it. But now he's around thirty, the snapping is getting worse, and he is drinking every day. He has moved into Earl's Court in London and is hanging around a drinking crowd. They only put up with him because he has some money, which he is quickly going through, as he buys drinks and smokes for the group. None of this group works, although Netta has had a few bit parts and thinks herself an actress. She is beautiful and George is *madly* in love with her. She treats him like dirt and one of his minds is busy planning her death. The other mind allows him to grovel and whine, fetch and tote, just to be near her. His life is miserable, and then, about halfway through the book, he rediscovers golf! He is good at it! Using borrowed clubs and playing a strange course he shoots a sixty-eight. This the first time out after years away from the game. He is euphoric. He has done something which is very difficult to do and done it well. He is somebody! Then, another snap, and, he's back to drinking. Only now he's carrying a golf club everywhere he goes.

Chapter 2

Dust Jacket Color Illustrations

One of the most exciting aspects of book collecting is the discovery of a scarce book, complete with its original dust jacket. The wonderful art work of their day makes these early jackets collectibles in their own right. This, combined with scarcity, contributes to the collector's fervor to acquire them. Few jackets from the early 1900's have survived. Prior to the invention of plastic protectors for dust jackets, some collectors and libraries threw them away when they began to wear.

The following 16 pages of color illustrations contain many very scarce dust jackets and paper-back original-printing cover's. There are also a number of most recent jackets which are still readily found in used book shops and dealers catalogs.

Where the first edition dust jacket was unobtainable, the next earliest is featured. Regrettable, an elusive few still remain to be uncovered - the search goes on!

Still elluding us are:

John Brand's Will
Tragedy At The Thirteenth
Murder On The Links
The Boomerange Clue
The Perilous Crossways
The Murder On The Sixth Hole
The Viaduct Murder
The Haunted Seventh

A short list of some of the scarcest jackets featured here:

The Nineteenth Hole Mystery	97
One To Play	97
Death On The First Tee	97

The SECRET of
BOGEY HOUSE
HERBERT ADAMS

THE GOLF HOUSE
BY MURDER
HERBERT ADAMS
AUTHOR OF THE CRIME IN THE DUTCH GARDEN
GUY

THE BODY
IN THE BUNKER
16

DEATH OFF THE
FAIRWAY
HERBERT ADAMS
CRIME CLUB

THE NINETEENTH
HOLE MYSTERY
HERBERT ADAMS

HERBERT ADAMS
One
to play

HERBERT ADAMS
Death
on
the
first Tee

A FIVE STAR ORIGINAL
MURDER in the
ROUGH
7
A FULL-LENGTH MYSTERY NOVEL
FIVE STAR MYSTERY
25¢
LESLIE ALLEN

MURDER
IN THE ROUGH
Horace Brown
HUMOUR AND HOMICIDE
7
1'6
BOARDMAN BOOKS

KILL ONE
KILL TWO
A MYSTERY STORY by
W. W. ANDERSON

Death of a
Low-Handicap
Man
BRIAN BALL
13
By the author of
Montenegrin Gold

Death Is a Two-Stroke Penalty
A HACKER MYSTERY
James Y. Bartlett

Death from the Ladies' Tee
A HACKER MYSTERY
James Y. Bartlett

TRENT'S
OWN
CASE
BY E·C·BENTLEY
AUTHOR OF TRENT'S LAST CASE
& H·WARNER ALLEN

THE NAKED
FAIRWAYS
Michael Borissow

SYDNEY BOX
Alibi in the
Rough

SEALED
AND DESPATCHED
FREDA BREAM
THRILLER

The Vicar
Investigates
Freda
Bream

The Country Club
A New Novel by
Nancy Bruff

THE CASE OF THE GREEN FELT HAT
CHRISTOPHER BUSH

13
the PRO-AM Murders
Photo fiction
by
Patrick Cake

VICTOR CANNING
THE LIMBO LINE

KILLER TAKE ALL
JAMES·O·CAUSEY

the 86 proof pro
Based on an idea by
Don MacCrossen
A Novel by
Philip & Florence Chabody
An exciting story of big-time golf, with three professional gamblers out to rig the Las Vegas Open

The Murder on the Links
By Agatha Christie
The Bodley Head Ninepenny Novels

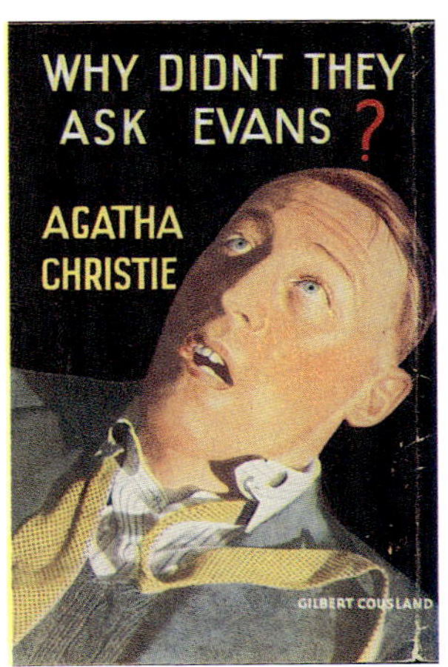
WHY DIDN'T THEY ASK EVANS?
AGATHA CHRISTIE
GILBERT COUSLAND

TOWARDS ZERO
AGATHA CHRISTIE

AGATHA
A new Mystery novel by
CHRISTIE
What Mrs. McGillicuddy Saw!

AGATHA CHRISTIE
4-50 FROM PADDINGTON
CRIME CLUB CHOICE

CAROLINE B. COONEY
SAND TRAP

DEAD BALL
A Mystery
Introducing Angus Straun
BARRY CORK

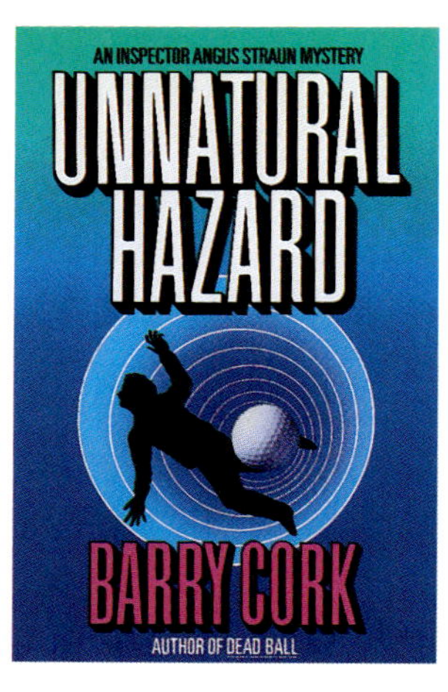
AN INSPECTOR ANGUS STRAUN MYSTERY
UNNATURAL HAZARD
BARRY CORK
AUTHOR OF DEAD BALL

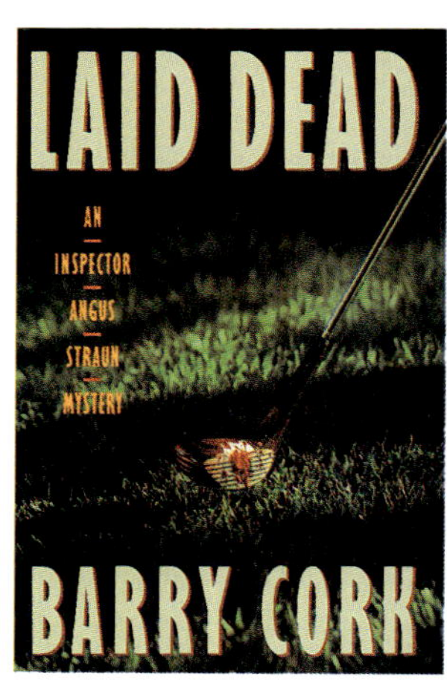
LAID DEAD
AN INSPECTOR ANGUS STRAUN MYSTERY
BARRY CORK

BARRY CORK
ENDANGERED SPECIES

AN INSPECTOR ANGUS STRAUN MYSTERY
WINTER
RULES
BARRY CORK

Iain Crawford
SCARE THE GENTLE CITIZEN

THE TANG MURDERS
Charles Cruickshank

LOCAL KNOWLEDGE
A Kieran Lenahan Mystery
CONOR DALY
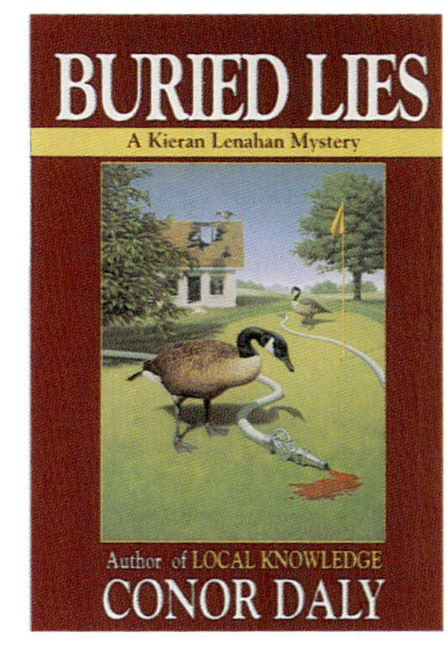
BURIED LIES
A Kieran Lenahan Mystery
Author of LOCAL KNOWLEDGE
CONOR DALY

UNEXPECTED
Night
A MYSTERY BY
Elizabeth Daly

COLLINS CRIME CLUB
Three Green Bottles
DOMINIC DEVINE
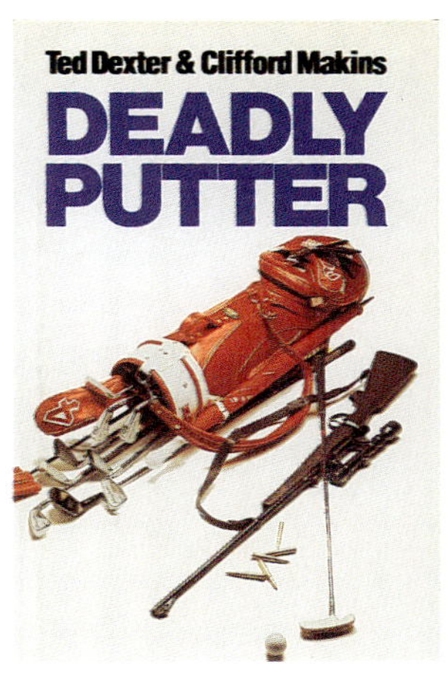
Ted Dexter & Clifford Makins
DEADLY PUTTER

CARTER DICKSON
My Late Wives

The BUNKER AT THE 5th
BY MARCUS DODS

THE DEADLY DIARY
William DuBois

142
A GRAPHIC MYSTERY
25c
FAIR PREY
WILL DUKE

FAIR PREY
Will Duke
AMERICAN MYSTERY

MATCH FOR A MURDERER
A NOVEL OF SUSPENSE
DOROTHY DUNNETT

FRANCIS DURBRIDGE
A GAME OF MURDER
START

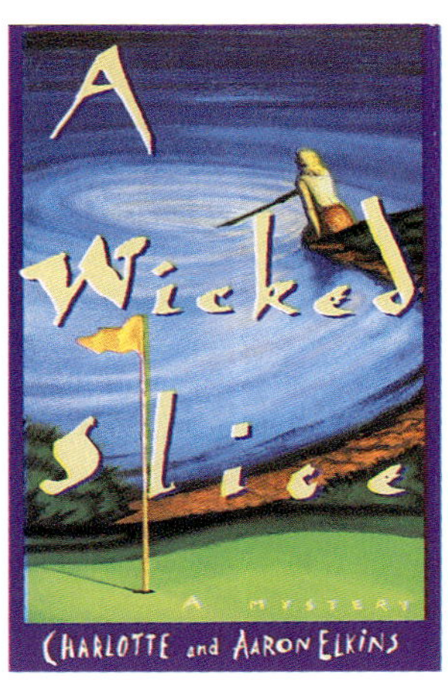
A Wicked Slice
A MYSTERY
CHARLOTTE and AARON ELKINS

Charlotte and Aaron
ELKINS
Rotten Lies

A TOUGH CALIFORNIA PRIVATE EYE PICKS UP A DEADLY GAME OF GOLF WHERE MURDER IS PAR FOR THE COURSE.
By the author of BLOOD ON THE MOON
"Fast paced and entertaining"
West Coast Review of Books
JAMES ELLROY
BROWN'S REQUIEM

JAMES ELLROY
BROWN'S REQUIEM
ALLISON & BUSBY

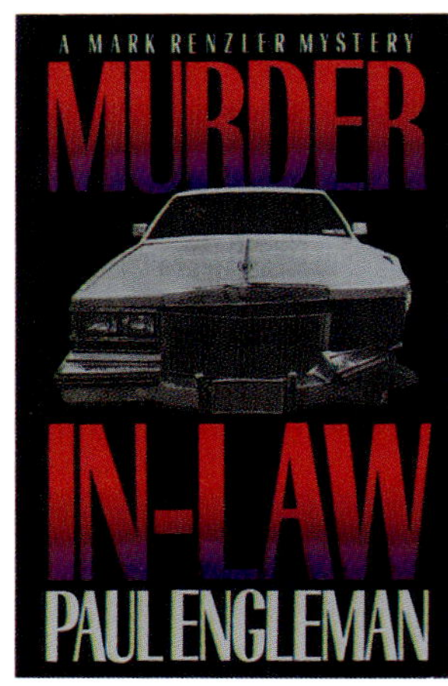
A MARK RENZLER MYSTERY
MURDER IN-LAW
PAUL ENGLEMAN

Mr MALCOLM PRESENTS
2nd
FAIRLIE's
Golfer-Detective Thrill

SHOT IN THE DARK
SICK WITH TERROR, THE OLD MAN REMAINED FOR AN ETERNITY OF SUSPENSE LISTENING ... AGAIN THAT SINISTER SHAFT ON THE CEILING WAS MOVING. A VIVID FLASH OF LIGHTNING LIT THE ROOM, BUT HE COULD SEE NO CROUCHING FORM, NO FIGURE HIDING IN THE SHADOWS. WITH A SHAKING HAND HE WIPED THE BEADS OF PERSPIRATION FROM HIS BROW, TURNED HIS ANGUISHED EYES .... WITHIN THE ROOM SOME ONE SUDDENLY LAUGHED.
FAIRLIE'S FIRST BIG GOLFER THRILL
FAIRLIE

MEN FOR COUNTERS
"They will attack when they've finished playing with us at dawn probably." "There is one chance we've got to take it and you're the one to go......" "No?" "Right, let's cut for it, lowest goes, highest stays, aces count high." "Cut".
FAIRLIE

THE SEVEN SLEEPERS
Elizabeth Ferrars
Constable
Crime

IAN FLEMING
GOLDFINGER

A MYSTERY NOVEL
TERROR TOURNAMENT
J. M. FLYNN

THE STRANGE DEATH OF MARTIN GREEN
BY
DAVID FROME
WHOSE FOOTPRINTS MARRED THE SEVENTH TEE?
A CRIME CLUB DETECTIVE STORY

Reunion with Murder
CLASS OF '31
HARVARD
Timothy Fuller
The new Jupiter Jones mystery by the author of HARVARD HAS A HOMICIDE

Teed Off!
NICOLA FURLONG

JONATHAN GRAY
The OWL

SUDDEN DEATH
James Gibbins

J. M. GREGSON
MURDER AT THE NINETEENTH
YONEX

J.M.GREGSON
DEAD ON COURSE

THE SILVER KING MYSTERY
18
IAN GREIG

DOROTHY HALLIDAY
Dolly and the Doctor Bird

MALCOLM HAMER
DEATH TRAP
A CHRIS LUDLOW GOLFING THRILLER

MALCOLM HAMER
A CHRIS LUDLOW GOLFING THRILLER
SUDDEN DEATH

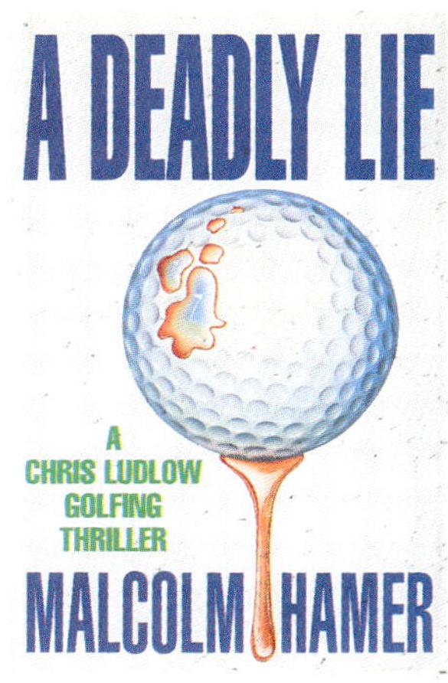
A DEADLY LIE
A CHRIS LUDLOW GOLFING THRILLER
MALCOLM HAMER

MALCOLM HAMER
SHADOWS ON THE GREEN
A CHRIS LUDLOW GOLFING THRILLER

MALCOLM HAMER
Dead on Line
A CHRIS LUDLOW GOLFING THRILLER

HANGOVER SQUARE
by
PATRICK HAMILTON

T.H.E
CLUB
J.A.N.E
HELLER

THE LOST GOLFER
by Horace G. Hutchinson

MARTIN INIGO
STONE DEAD
When golf becomes a killing game...

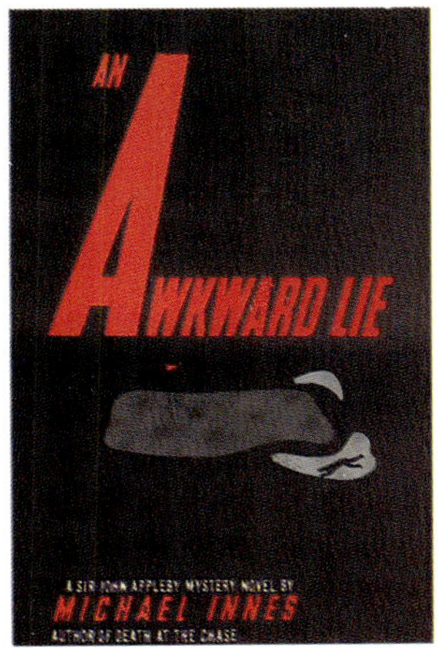
AN AWKWARD LIE
A SIR JOHN APPLEBY MYSTERY NOVEL BY
MICHAEL INNES
AUTHOR OF DEATH AT THE CHASE

QUINTIN JARDINE
SKINNER'S ROUND

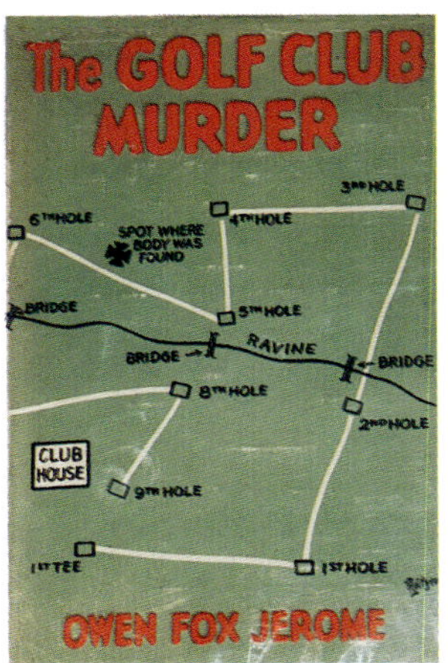
The GOLF CLUB MURDER
6TH HOLE
SPOT WHERE BODY WAS FOUND
4TH HOLE
3RD HOLE
BRIDGE
5TH HOLE
RAVINE
BRIDGE
BRIDGE
8TH HOLE
2ND HOLE
CLUB HOUSE
9TH HOLE
1ST TEE
1ST HOLE
OWEN FOX JEROME

H.R.F. KEATING
THE BODY IN THE BILLIARD ROOM

BY JERRY KENNEALY
POLO IN THE ROUGH
A NICK POLO MYSTERY

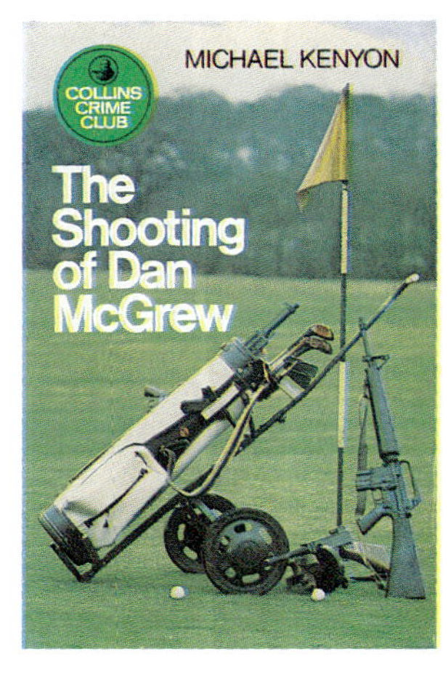
COLLINS CRIME CLUB
MICHAEL KENYON
The Shooting of Dan McGrew

THE KILLING GAME
A CRIME CLUB SELECTION BY BILL KNOX

A NEW NOVEL OF SUSPENSE BY THE AUTHOR OF
THE SHADOW OF THE PALMS AND UNDER ORION
DEATH UNDER PAR
Janice Law

A Captain Heimrich Mystery
Murder Can't Wait
Richard Lockridge

A novel of suspense at the U.S. Open
Follow the Leader
JOHN LOGUE

A MORRIS AND SULLIVAN MYSTERY
MURDER ON THE LINKS
JOHN LOGUE
You haven't lived until you've died at Augusta National...

MURDER AT THE OPEN
ANGUS MACVICAR

THE
HAMMERS
OF
FINGAL
Angus MacVicar

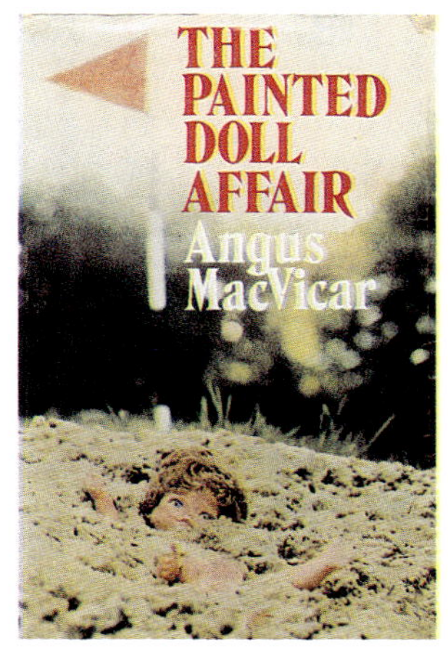
THE
PAINTED
DOLL
AFFAIR
Angus
MacVicar

60¢ A FLAGSHIP SPY THRILLER
A Deadly
Game
By Will Manson
A violent impact explodes the ball
off the tee, and a deadly and
dangerous game begins.

COVER
HER
FACE
Hugh McCutcheon

BRAND FOR
THE BURNING
HUGH
McCUTCHEON

Lying
Three
A
Father Dowling
Mystery by
Ralph McInerny

An Andrew Broom Mystery
CAUSE
AND
EFFECT
RALPH McINERNY

An Andrew Broom Mystery
BODY
AND
SOIL
RALPH McINERNY

LAW AND ARDOR
AN ANDREW BROOM MYSTERY
RALPH McINERNY
AUTHOR OF MOM AND DEAD

THE VICAR IN HELL
ALAN MELVILLE
AUTHOR OF "QUICK CURTAIN"

BULLET HOLE
KEITH MILES

DOUBLE EAGLE
A NOVEL BY
KEITH MILES

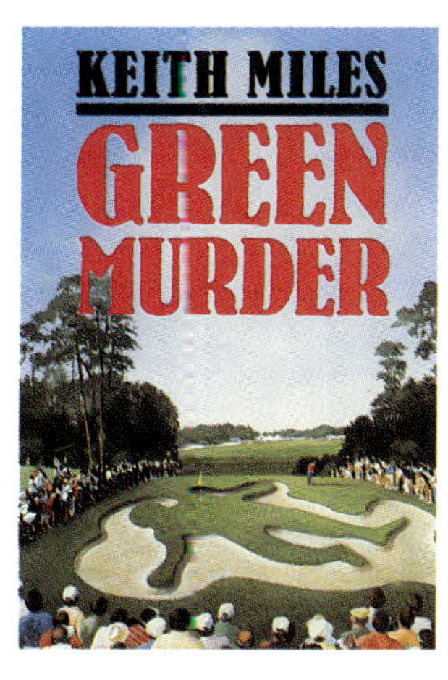
KEITH MILES
GREEN MURDER

KEITH MILES
FLAGSTICK

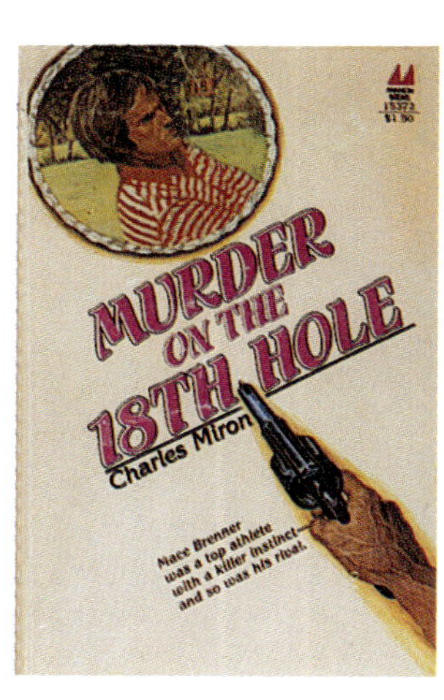
MURDER ON THE 18TH HOLE
Charles Miron
Nace Brenner was a top athlete with a killer instinct—and so was his rival.

TO KILL A COCONUT
Patricia Moyes

THE GLASSY POND
E. WRIGHT MOXLEY
AUTHOR of:
"RED SNOW"

The Obituary Arrives At Two O'clock
Japan's Bestselling Mystery Writer
Shizuko Natsuki
Author of
THE THIRD LADY
In a wealthy Tokyo suburb, a wrong number gives the signal for murder.

CASSELL CRIME
NOW LYING DEAD
OLIVE NORTON

JUST THE
FAX, MA'AM
A MOLLY MASTERS MYSTERY
GIRLS
LESLIE O'KANE

O CHARITABLE DEATH
RACHEL COSGROVE PAYES
A CRIME CLUB SELECTION

W. R. Philbrick
Slow Dancer
A Connie Kale Investigation

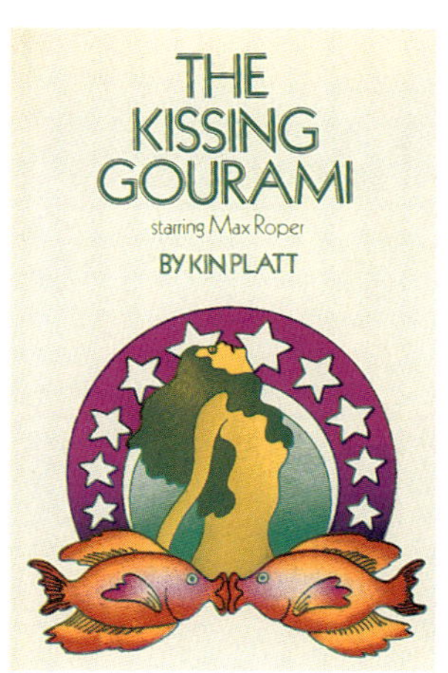
THE
KISSING
GOURAMI
starring Max Roper
BY KIN PLATT

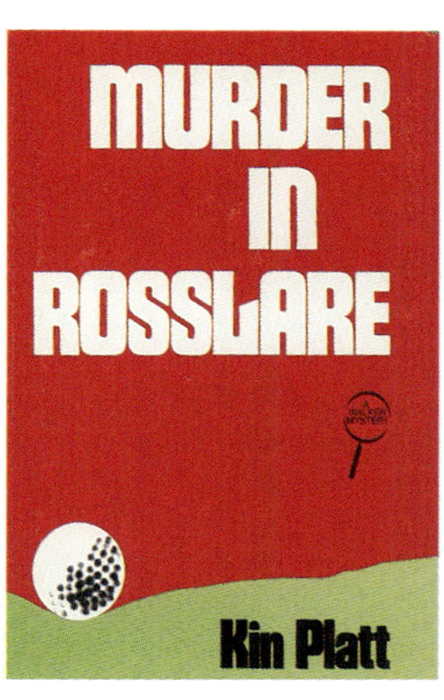
MURDER
IN
ROSSLARE
Kin Platt

"THE MOST INTRIGUING DETECTIVE . . . SINCE TRAVIS McGEE."
If I Should Die before I Wake
BY JERRY ALLEN POTTER

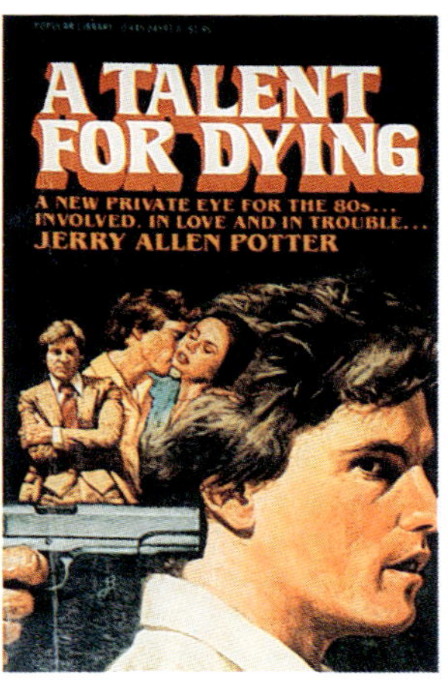
A TALENT
FOR DYING
A NEW PRIVATE EYE FOR THE 80s...
INVOLVED, IN LOVE AND IN TROUBLE...
JERRY ALLEN POTTER

THE GOLF LINKS
MYSTERY
PIERRE
QUIROULE

suspicion
LEE
ROBERTS

Passion and Intrigue at the British Open
William Rocke
OPERATION
BIRDIE

A GAME OF
SUDDEN DEATH
DOUGLAS RUTHERFORD

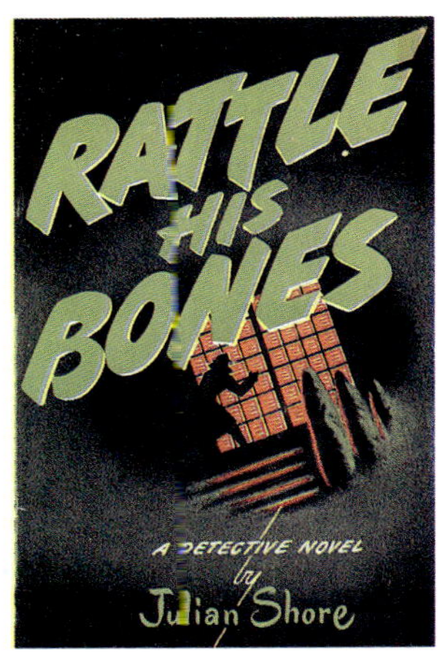
RATTLE
HIS
BONES
A DETECTIVE NOVEL
by
Julian Shore

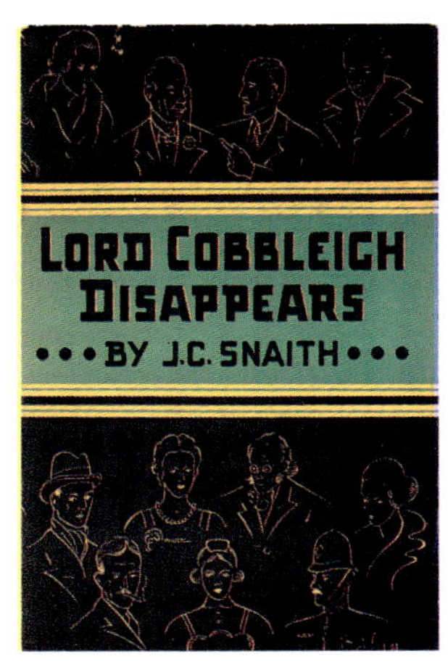
LORD COBBLEIGH
DISAPPEARS
BY J.C. SNAITH

CURIOUSER
AND
CURIOUSER
?
J.C. SNAITH
Author of "BUT EVEN SO"

The
GOLF COURSE
MYSTERY
Chester K. Steele

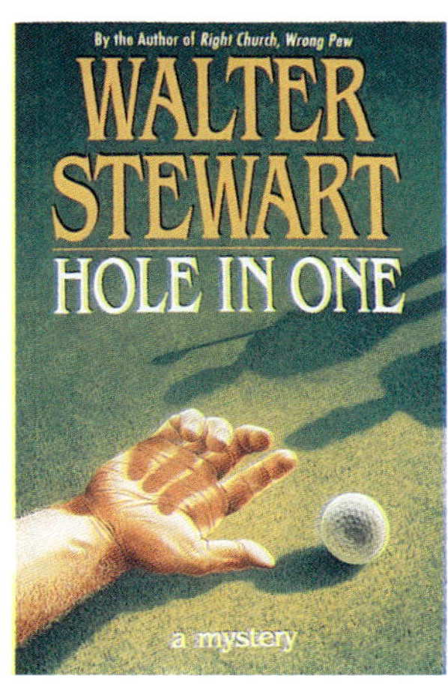
By the Author of Right Church, Wrong Pew
WALTER
STEWART
HOLE IN ONE
a mystery

MEET NERO WOLFE
FER-DE-LANCE
By the author of THE RUBBER BAND
By
REX
STOUT

THE MARSTON MURDER CASE
BY
WILLIAM·AVERILL·STOWELL

IAN STUART
SAND TRAP

THE CLUE of the CLEVER CANINE
Lee Tyler

SUCH FRIENDS ARE DANGEROUS
WALTER TYRER
STAPLES

ROBERT UPTON
DEAD ON THE STICK
AN AMOS McGUFFIN MYSTERY

UNHOLY WRIT
David Williams

David Williams
WEDDING TREASURE

Meet Michael Thompson, ace investigator, as he takes two harrowing trips into the brutal and terrifying world of murder.
THE TARTAN MURDERS
2 BOOKS IN 1
$10.00 VALUE FOR $5.95
MISSION BAY MURDER
PHILIP CARLTON WILLIAMS

DEATH OF A GOLFER
ANTHONY WYNNE

ANTHONY WYNNE'S
25 CENTS No. 14
MURDER
IN THE MORNING
A Detective Novel CLASSIC
COMPLETE AND UNABRIDGED

A QUINN PARKER NOVEL OF SUSPENSE
CRIMSON GREEN
BRUCE ZIMMERMAN

THE PERFECT ROUND
HERBERT ADAMS
AUTHOR OF 'THE SECRET OF BOGEY HOUSE'

TRENT INTERVENES
E.C. BENTLEY

MURDER IN THE MEWS
AGATHA CHRISTIE
4 Poirot Stories

SHERLOCK HOLMES, THE GOLFER
by
Bob Jones

DEATH BALL
AND OTHER STORIES
BY
ENOCH REES

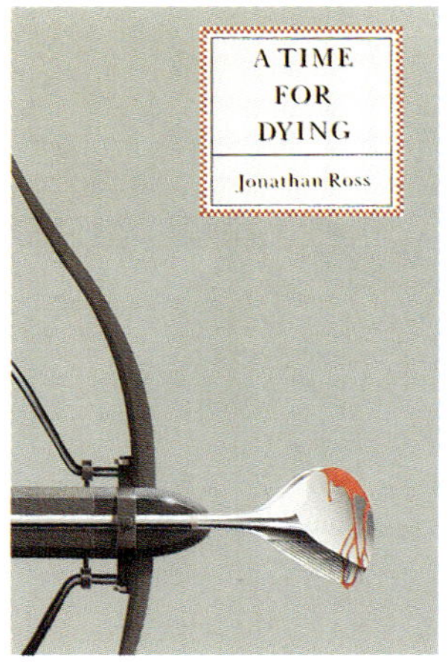
A TIME FOR DYING
Jonathan Ross

Michael Underwood
A PARTY TO MURDER
3

Heller, Jane, US,
THE CLUB
Kensington Books, New York, 1995, 266 pages, 23.5 cm

Maybe this book is a put-on. The bright pink dust jacket may be a clue that this book, despite a murder and a detective, is not a mystery but a new kind of romance novel. It's uncertain if the author is *dead* serious about murder. Finish this book, or you will miss the strangest piece of police work ever. (Tip: The local police have a sure-fire suicide-prevention program). Golf is talked throughout but few shots are played.

Judy, Hunt's wife, is resisting his proposition that their new membership in The Oaks Country Club will help him obtain clients for his brokerage firm. He argues that she can also network at the Club, seeking a job in publishing to replace the one she was recently fired from. Hunt loves golf and the Club. Judy has never played golf and very little tennis, and she hates the Club.

Judy's opinion of the Club changes completely when Claire Cox, America's foremost feminist, breaks the Club's iron-clad rule against admitting single women. Judy buys tennis clothes and goes to meet her idol. They hit it off.

They soon are busy at work, planning a book which Judy will ghost-write for Claire. Judy is devastated when her new friend and idol is murdered on the golf course with a wedge and her body left in a green-side bunker.

Judy is recruited by the police detective handling the case to be his inside person at the Club. Judy's decision to assist the police is not based 100 percent on doing ones civic duty. She and Hunt are drifting apart, and Detective Tom, is a young, virile widower. Judy is having sexual fantasies about Tom.

Over at the club there's lots of sex. There is sex in the bushes by the tennis courts and more in the parking lot. Completing this drama, another woman is beaten, slips into a coma and a policeman she has never met sits by her hospital bed ever day, falling in love with her. Sigh!

The answers are found on the golf course.

Hutchinson, Horace Gordon, British, 1859 - 1932
THE LOST GOLFER
John Murray, London, 1930, 335 pages, 19 cm

Of his nearly twenty mysteries, the author wrote only one known to contain anything regarding golf. That's strange, because Hutchinson is one of the foundation writers of golf literature. He did serious works on golf history, course construction, and analysis of the great players of his day. No golf library is complete without a representative collection of Hutchinson.

The Lost Golfer could be described as a whimsical, romantic mystery. There is no murder, but the list of crimes include two cases of kidnapping, gun running, and smuggling. The story is light, silly, and thoroughly delightful. Not a great deal of golf is played, but it is constantly talked about.

The hero/bumpkin, Galfred Frost, is a lazy young lawyer who only manages to keep his position in a famous London firm by bringing in cases from his upper-crust relatives. He prefers to spend his time playing golf. When his golf game goes sour, he copes by going fishing.

Galfred's unrequited love for the wife of a second cousin gets him into constant trouble. The young lady really is not such a lady, and she works Galfred like a yo-yo as she involves him in her schemes. Galfred is completely unaware that the relationship is obvious to everyone, including the husband. It is possible that he might have been able to figure it out if he was not otherwise totally occupied, going through a horrid spell of "socketing his mashie" (shanking his irons), which wholly precludes consideration of any other problem.

If anyone ever did talk, as they do in this story, they no longer do. But it makes no difference. Make the effort to find and read this book, if only to get an entirely new slant on Hutchinson.

***Ingio, Martin,* pseudonym of Keith Miles**
STONE DEAD
Sphere Books Limited, London, 1991, 244 pages, paperback original

Murders, blackmail, sex, and lots of high-tension tournament golf, neatly mixed around the Ryder Cup matches, combine to make this one of the our favorite books in *The Golf Murders.*

The Ryder Cup, a three-day series of team matches, is completely different from professional golf tournaments that pit individual golfers against all the others and penalize a player for seeking advice on how to play a shot.

In the Ryder Cup, teams of the best professionals from the United States compete against the best from the United Kingdom and Europe. Each team has a leader-coach, also a professional golfer. They play, not for individual cash prizes, but for national honor.

In this story, the Ryder Cup is being played in England this year, with Don Hawker, sportswriter, covering the matches. Hawker knows first-hand about the stress and concentration required of the competitors in any world-class sports competition. He was a great track star and still runs almost every day, for fun and to relax.

Hawker books a room at a country guest house, not far from the matches. Checking in, he notices a pair of field glasses on the window sill of his second-story room. Looking out over the farm next door, he notices something off-color sticking out of a manure collection lagoon.

Adjusting the focus, he sees the object jump into the lenses. It is a human hand, sticking up as though to grab or catch something. Next to it, on top of the slime, is a white golf ball. After the police are called but before they arrive, Hawker goes down to the pond and retrieves the ball. On it are the initials of the current American Superstar golfer. Hawker does not give the ball to the police - he has an attitude about police! While obtaining his press credentials at the tournament, he learns the PR Director is an old friend of his recently deceased wife. After a few hesitant meetings, they begin a tentative relationship. Hawker asks around about the body and the ball from the pond, and someone responds by trying to kill him with a shovel. There is a second killing, and again Hawker is first on the scene. The police are not pleased.

***Innes, Michael,* British, 1906 - 1995, pseudonym of John I.M. Stewart**
AN AWKWARD LIE
Gollancz, London, 1971, 192 pages, 21 cm
Dodd, Mead, New York, 1971, 192 pages, 21 cm

This is another book in which the golf connection is limited to the shot which found the bunker and the body already occupying it. While this is certainly enough for inclusion here, the reader is also sure to enjoy this story. The author, universally acknowledged as "a witty and erudite writer of suspense novels," presents a classic cozy with a satisfying conclusion.

The following description is taken from the inside front dust jacket flap.

"Michael Innes is at his entertaining best in this superbly inventive tale of a disappearing corpse. Bobby, that engaging son of that great master of detection, Sir John Appleby, found the body. He was having an early round of golf on his own, when he hit his ball into a bunker and saw a dead man lying there, shot in the head.

"While he was wondering what to do, a very attractive and level headed girl arrived on the scene - a girl who immediately impressed the susceptible Bobby. He went back to the club house to telephone for the police, but when he returned with Sergeant Howard, there was no girl and no corpse. All that remained of his story was his ball, still in the bunker. 'Mr. Appleby,' Sergeant Howard remarked, 'you seem to be in rather an awkward lie.'

"The police were at first inclined to regard Bobby's story as a youthful practical joke. But he had a clue, and in following it up, wandered into a sinister yet hilariously comic mystery."

Jardine, Quintin, Scotland
SKINNER'S ROUND
Headline, London, 1995, 311 pages, 24 cm

The golf is a banquet, every hole a luscious dish, and each shot delicious.

Three good women, living in Gullane, East Lothian, were burned as witches in 1598. They were accused by the local Laird, The Earl of Kinture, of causing a terrible storm in Aberlady Bay. The storm nearly sank the ship of King James VI, who was passing by. Legend has Agnes Tod, one of the women, calling down a curse on any who desecrate the hill they died on. Witches Hill it has been known since, and few go there.

Witches Hill Golf and Country Club, built by the current Earl of Kinture, is lavish - and talk about location! It is between Aberlady and Muirfield Golf Course, just a full wedge to Archie Baird's golf museum. The Club's "coming out" is to be a tournament featuring eight of the world's best professionals, each teamed with three amateurs. The pro's will be playing for one million pounds sterling, put up by Japan's Murano Motors.

Two days before the start, Michael White, the Earl's partner in Witches Hill, is murdered. He is found in his hot tub following a practice round on the course, with his throat cut. The police lack clues until a note arrives at a local newspaper, citing Agnes Tod's curse: "the first will die by the blade."

Two days later, a body is found lashed into the course's antique witches' dunking chair. A second note left at another newspaper says, "the second by water." Of course, fire gets the third, and you will not believe what the witches(?) do to the last one.

the past couple of years. They play four rounds, under sun, rain, and wind, making every kind of shot. Savor this one!.

***Jerome, Owen Fox*, 1897 - 1963, pseudonym of , Oscar Jerome Friend**

THE GOLF CLUB MURDER

Edward Clode, New York, 1929, 319 pages, 19 cm

THE GOLF COURSE MURDER

Hutchinson, London, 1928, 319 pages, 19 cm

This is a mystery, an action story, and a romance, all done up in proper cozy fashion. The first of two murders is committed on the course, during a round, in a very different way. There is not much golf, but it is central to the story.

Note: We have never seen the British printing of this title.

John Hardy is back in West Fork less than ten minutes before he is in a fight. Walking up the main street, he intervenes when two men attempt to physically drag a pretty young woman out of her auto, which is parked next to the courthouse.

When the fight ends, John is handcuffed and thrown in jail. He learns that he has assaulted the town's city attorney and prosecuting attorney, as well as the three police officers they called in as reinforcements. He finds out later from a friendly jailer that the woman is the daughter of the local newspaper editor, who is in the same jail, charged with the murder of the town's leading banker. John is not even a little saddened by banker Fosdick's death. Fosdick and his rich cronies, who run the town, had destroyed John's father, leading to the father's suicide ten years ago. John left town then, but is back now, very rich and eager for revenge.

also alone, at 8 a.m. Wright came back to the clubhouse, disheveled and dirty, about an hour later and left the course. Fosdick's body was found in the sixth fairway that afternoon.

John learns golf from Wright's daughter so that he can better clear her father of the murder. At the same time he is agitating the town's elite, and they are starting to turn on each other.

Keating, H.R.F., British, 1926 -, *Evelyn Hervey*

THE BODY IN THE BILLIARD ROOM

Hutchinson, London, 1987, 247 pages, 22 cm

Viking, New York, 1987, 21.5 cm

The author used golf in the manner of Herbert Adams, to reveal a little of the character of the player which might otherwise be carefully controlled and hidden from others. Inspector Ghote is unique and the location is fascinating. This is a fun read.

Inspector Ghote of the Bombay India Police is assigned to a murder case in a resort town, high in the cool hills of Southern India. The town is reminiscent of Old Victorian England, but slowly going to seed. Ghote finds that he has been specifically requested - someone there thinks him one of the "great detectives" like those featured in books by Christie and Doyle.

The suspects are a handful of ancient whites and merely elderly Indians who have retired from the civil service or professions. All are trying to hold onto a time long passed everywhere else. All seems very proper, but it is known that the murder victim was a small-time blackmailer, and he may have had one or more of them in his portfolio.

Ghote's investigation technique involves starting a conversation with each of the suspects, without appearing to interrogate them. However, the only way to get any time with one suspect is to play golf with him. Ghote has never swung a club, but he goes, determined to watch his playing partner and do as he does. This lasts for two holes,during which Ghote reveals a latent talent for world-class golf.

Inspector Ghote, self-deprecating and charming, is also very shrewd. Suspects at their leisure are more likely to make revealing disclosures.

Kennealy, Jerry, US, *G.P. Kennealy*

POLO IN THE ROUGH

St. Martin's Press, New York, 1989, 181 pages, 21.5 cm

The pro-am scene is the heart of the plot, but no golf is played in the book. The title and the dust jacket illustration combine with The Crosby to squeak this one in.

Jack Slate writes a book about the CIA that names secret agents. Three of them are killed in a few months time. Slate writes a number of other high-profile exposés, and they all make the best-seller list. They also make him a pile of enemies.

Now he is working on a book about the enormous wealth the Shah Of Iran took out of his country and, what happened to it after his death. His publisher, concerned that someone will kill him (before they get the finished manuscript) hires private detective Nick Polo to guard him.

Slate's celebrity as a writer gets him invited to play in prestigious pro-ams. A couple of weeks earlier, he played in the Hope in Palm Springs. This week, he is in the biggy, The Crosby at Caramel. He finishes up at Pebble Beach.

Actually, he crashes his two-seater plane into the seventeenth fairway, early on the morning of the first practice round. Polo watches him take off, a camera with a long zoom lens in his hand. A few minutes later, the crash news of Slate's death is on Polo's car radio.

Polo notifies the publisher's lawyer and gets new orders. Find the manuscript, quick! Back at Slate's house, he is just starting to search when the local sheriff, and the FBI arrive, and he is arrested for burglary. The publisher's lawyer gets him out, but the officers are not pleased.

Another private detective comes looking for the manuscript. Polo intercepts him and runs him off. However, the next morning the other detective's body is found in a garage. The wife of a CIA man, working with Slate on the book, is found shot in her home.

Polo finds some pictures of the Hope pro-am. A CIA man, Slate, and a former Iranian official are all in golf togs. The connection must be golf, and Polo heads back to The Crosby for the answers.

Kenyon, Michael, British, 1931 -, *Daniel Forbes*
THE SHOOTING OF DAN McGREW
Collins Crime Club, London 1972, 191 pages, 20 cm
David McKay, New York, 1975, 191 pages, 21 cm

There is not a single stroke of golf in this story, but the final scene on a golf course, along with the wonderfully graphic dust jacket illustration on the Collins printing, combine to make it a must for this collection.

Ogden Enterprises has a geological exploration going in Carrigann, Ireland. The first two geologists dispatched from the home office in Toronto are now missing. Even though the initial exploration report indicates sufficient quantities of valuable minerals at depths that make mining them worth going after, Skipper Ogden, the corporation head, is thinking of closing the site down.

But first, Skipper sends Henry Butt to investigate the disappearances and report back. Henry has no particular skills beyond his professional training as a geologist and a high proficiency for selecting the correct wine with dinner. Henry arrives in Ireland and gets settled into his guest house in Carrigann.

The first evening, he meets a nice Irish lass who is spending the last of her savings at the resort, looking for a husband. Henry invites her to dinner, and they share a bottle of wine. After dinner, on his way to his room (alone), he is hit, very hard, on the head. A further attempt on his life results in his being assigned protection by the local police.

Spotting the lady he dined with, in a neighboring village, he runs after her. His police escort lingers behind. As Henry catches up to the lady, a car with a gunman drives by, shooting at them. Later, in the police escort car, they are ambushed at the geology site. The car is destroyed and the officer driving it is killed.

The resourceful lady catches a local farmer's horse, and the two of them mount up and set off for the resort hotel. Chased all through the night by the killers, they arrive at the resort golf course just before dawn. They are forced to hide in a sand trap as the bad guys are between them and the hotel. A gun battle ensues; a man is skewered with the flag stick from the home hole.

Knox, Bill (William), Scotland, 1928 -

Noah Webster, Michael Kirk, Robert MacLeod

THE KILLING GAME

Doubleday CC, New York, 1963, 178 pages, 21.5 cm

THE MAN IN THE BOTTLE

John Long, London, 1963, 184 pages,

The story takes place in Scotland, with the action culminating in *The Old Gray Town* (St Andrews). There, a man is imprisoned in the bottle dungeon, in the castle ruins, that border the golf course. There is very little golf in this one, but what there is, is played on out the *Old Course.*

Another interesting golf-related murder device is introduced, not exactly the exploding ball-washer we have been waiting for, but can it be long until it is worked into a plot?

From the dust jacket blurb; *Two men had gone fishing - apparently with dynamite. Now one of the would-be poachers was dead, the other missing. At first Chief Inspector Thane, of the Glasgow Police, saw no connection between this case and his complicated assignment to guard a visiting Russian General.*

But when four Russian sailors were accused of stealing explosives from a colliery near where the greedy fisherman's body had been found and the General narrowly escaped death from a bomb. Thane realized that he would have to act quickly to prevent the unsporting killer from catching a very big fish indeed."

Knox, Ronald, British, 1888 - 1957

THE VIADUCT MURDER

Methuen, London, 1925, 252 pages, 19 cm

Simon and Schuster, NY, 1926,

This is the first of six mysteries written by the author, a Catholic Priest and, noted church scholar. He was reputedly advised to discontinue this sideline and he obeyed. His mysteries are highly regarded and collected. The dust jacket for this title is rarely seen.

In northern England, two tiny villages on opposite hillsides face each other across a valley. The railroad is carried across the valley on a viaduct, and under the viaduct is the golf course. From the third tee, the railroad stretches into the distance, paralleling the course on the right. Ahead is the great viaduct that spans laboriously in four giant arches over the little River Gudgeon. Shallow and narrow the river runs, fringed by willows, a paddling place for cows and for unoccupied caddies. Here and there it throws out patches of weeds, much dreaded by golfers.

Now on the course are the quintessential British gentleman's foursome, having been stuck in the clubhouse all day by rain showers and, now hurrying to get in a late afternoon round. Almost certainly, one of four will hit a slice off the tee, and so it is that a search begins for a lost ball. The search finds a man's body in the weeds at the foot of the viaduct. The fall from the tracks above made identification impossible.

While waiting for the caddie to bring the local constable, the foursome inexplicably decide to search the body and vicinity for clues. They find a few items and, even more inexplicably, withhold them from the police. Within a few days, the death is ruled a suicide. The foursome know other-wise and continue to investigate.

There is much talk of the golf they are missing while conducting their unauthorized investigation, but little more is played. A map opposite the title page helps.

Law, Janice, US, 1941
DEATH UNDER PAR
Houghton Mifflin Co., New York, 1981, 234 pages, 21.5 cm
Houghton, London, 1982,

Without diminishing the golf sequences, the author shows us The Old Grey Toon in lovely detail. St. Andrews University, (the oldest in Britain), the castle and cathedral ruins, and the ancient pier all made this a desirable vacation destination, even for the non-golfer.

Anna Peters owns and manages her own security firm. Not securities, as in stocks and bonds, but the private investigation kind. The business is located in Washington, D.C., where in July the weather is unbearable. Things are really slow and Harry, the recently acquired replacement husband, gets a great idea. He is a free-lance commercial artist who has just landed a commission to paint a series of watercolors of the 1978 British Open. The Open is to be at St. Andrews, Scotland. They agree this could be the honeymoon they didn't have. Anna is blessed with an infinitely competent office manager, allowing her to travel without worry.

Anna and Harry are just nicely getting settled in St. Andrews when Anna gets a call from a former client. The man is a US businessman who is a member of the Royal and Ancient (R&A), golf's ruling body in Great Britain. The R&A's concern is the Open. It is to start in a few days on the Old Course, and someone has been vandalizing the course.

Anna agrees to investigate. But the next day, her role is expanded when the current American golfing star receives a death threat. The American star ignores the threat and obstinately refuses to cooperate with Anna. Undeterred by his bullheadedness, or a street attack on her the next night, she uncovers a set of strange coincidences.

Three people, the golfer, an American land developer who was just murdered in Tayside near St. Andrews, and a university professor who was run down in a traffic accident the day before, are all graduates of the same small college in New England. There had been a terrible robbery in the college town while they were students. Three people were murdered and a priceless coin collection stolen. The three Americans each wear a piece of jewelry made from antique coins.

Lockridge, Richard, US, 1898 - 1982, *Francis Richards*
MURDER CAN'T WAIT

Lippincott Co., Philadelphia, 1964, 189 pages, 21.5 cm

The dust jacket has a nice *Country Clubish* illustration with golf featured. In the story, a murder investigation takes place largely in a bar at a country club. This, the dust jacket, and the fact that the club golf pro is one of the prime murder suspects, constitute the golf connection. The author was a very big name in the field thirty years ago. The author's pseudonym was used for the British printing.

The following is from the dust jacket:

The football that Stuart Fleming used to carry when he was at Dyckman University was never more up in the air that Lt. Nathan Shapiro is here. Fleming, laid up with a broken leg at his Westchester County home, calls the Manhattan police with a story of gamblers trying to get at the current Dyckman football squad for point-shaving purposes. Shapiro drives out to the country to question him, only to discover that someone handy with a gun has been there first. The handsome ex-football star is deader that a punctured pigskin.

That's when Captain Heimrich gets into the game, and discovers that football isn't the only sport involved. There's golf, for instance, and philandering, in various directions possibly involving a blonde named Enid, or a black-haired secretary called Catherine, or a redheaded Mrs. Isabel Bryce, widow, or all three.

At the right moment, and not one moment too soon, Heimrich and Shapiro run a couple of fast plays and combine strategy for a finish that will leave the fans cheering.

***Loder, Vernon*, British, 1881-, Pseudonym of John George Haslette Vahey**
SUSPICION
Collins Crime Club, London, 1933, 252 pages, 19 cm

Although there is not a lot of golf after the first couple of chapters, it is essential to the plot and well described. The story is interesting, but the author disappoints by cheating at the end.

Julius Hennessy is spending a great deal of time on the golf links with the pretty young wife of Mr. Holt, an elderly solicitor. While Julius and Bessie Holt are playing golf, Julius's wife Hetty is spending every available minute fishing. Her fishing companion is the handsome and unmarried Bill French, who is also Julius's cousin.

The members of the Martley Golf Club and the townspeople of Martley in general have much to gossip about, especially when it becomes known that Julius has spoken sternly to his wife about being alone with French for long hours, and she still refuses to give up her fishing with him.

All of this is observed with interest by Mr. Brown, a stranger recently arrived in Martley. Brown has purchased a month's playing privilege at the golf club. Within a short time, he is playing regularly with Julius, Bessie, and others in their group. Mr. Brown speaks little of himself, but it is known that he fancies himself a criminologist, and he has long conversations with the local police inspector on the subject.

Julius is murdered! His body is found on the wooded river bank near Bessie's favorite fishing spot. The exact location is within sight of Bill French's home on the other bank. Julius is found at night by police after Bessie notifies them that he has not come home for dinner. His car, found first, is parked where it would be a short walk through the woods to the river. A pair of field glasses lying near Julius's body fuels speculation that Julius was attempting to spy on his wife and French.

Logue, John, US, 1933 -,

Logue has been a police reporter, a reporter for United Press, and a sportswriter at the *Atlanta Journal* for ten years. He learned under Ed Miles, once president of the American Golf Writers. Logue's character, John Morris, mirrors much of Miles' love of golf. Morris is featured in all Logue mysteries. The first, **Follow the Leader**, and the latest, **Murder on the Links**, are golf mysteries. There are two others, both are football stories.

Logue has another golf mystery in the works. Set at the British Open in St. Andrews, it is to be called **The Feathery Touch of Death**.

FOLLOW THE LEADER

Crown Publishing, New York, 1979, 210 pages, 23.5 cm

The reader can smell the fresh cut grass of the course, the stale smoke and sweat in the locker room, and the tension in the USGA and PGA meeting rooms. Many real-world famous-tour players, thinly disguised, are depicted in this story. The relationships and tension among the players, even without murders to complicate things, make this one of the best. It is also chock full of great golf.

The U.S. Open is being played in Atlanta. Many of the players, media, and tour officials, are staying at the Peachtree Towers Hotel with its twenty-one-story lobby. John Morris, sportswriter for The Associated Press, is registered there.

On Wednesday evening, Morris is killing time in the lobby and decides to ride, with three of the pros, in the glass-sided elevator up to a party. On the way up, they pass Jim Rossi, TV color commentator and legendary golf teacher, standing on the balcony, looking like he is waiting for someone.

Morris only stays a few minutes at the party and then takes the elevator back down. Rossi, arms wind-milling in space, passes the elevator on its way down. Morris is an eye witness, at least to the part of Rossi's flight from just below his balcony to the lobby floor below.

The next evening in the players' locker room, Morris tries to help John Whitlow, the tour's current blazing rocket, and the first-day tournament leader. Whitlow's putter, the only one he has ever used, is missing, and he is frantic. He and Morris look in the press tent and the bag storage room. Whitlow then trots off to the seventeenth green to see if he left the putter there (he had chipped in from off the green on the last hole).

The next moring, Whitlow is pulled out of the pond at the seventeenth green. The police say he was in the water all night. Deciding not to cancel the tournament, the USGA relizes an even worse mightmare, the Friday leader is also murdered.

MURDER ON THE LINKS

Dell Publishing, NY, 1996, 323 pages, paperback original

This book is a real keeper. It is not on my personal ten-best list only because **Follow The Leader** by Logue is already there. Logue uses the pros' real names this time, and the golf scenes would cause Darwin to blink away a happy tear.

Morris is back in Atlanta, this time for the Masters and a pre-tournament memorial party for Monty Sullivan, former Masters winner and late husband of Julia, Morris's Lady Love. Morris has aged gracefully and is retired form the AP, and Julia has simply grown more beautiful.

The morning after the party, and the day before the first practice round, Morris and Julia walk the course and stop at Eisenhower Pond. There, at the pond's edge, in exactly the same place where Cliff Roberts' body fell when he shot himself years ago, is Melvin Newton's body. Newton, variously known as Augusta National Club Member, The Thousand-Dollar Suit, and Cheap Bastard, has a bullet hole in his head and a pistol in his hand.

The next day, following the practice round, the most detested man among the golfing elite, is stabbed to death and left in a Port-O-Let behind the tenth green. The third man murdered, but not until the Masters is over, is last years champion and a complete jerk.

The exciting finish is pure magic. The winner's final nine-hole charge is detailed, birdie after sparkling birdie. When not counting bodies or birdies, Morris discovers a major art talent. A former touring pro, whose career ended when arthritis crippled his hands, has secretly painted for years. He mentions to Morris a collection of portraits of Julia, going back twenty-five years. From this, the reader is treated to a short and very interesting art appreciation segment.

MacVicar, Angus, Scotland, 1908 -

The author's lowest handicap was six, perhaps not spectacular, but it was only thirteen when he reached age 75. No recent handicap has been posted for this young 88 year old. His home course, Dunavery GC in Argyll, is fondly described as the course in Pittendall on Scotland's west coast.

A writer all his working life, he was first a journeyman newspaper columnist. He also wrote young adult novels, science fiction, golf non-fiction, and a number of mysteries. Three mysteries are featured here, all with superb golf sequences in them.

While these three golf murders were written only as recently as between 1962 and 1975, they are quite difficult to find in Britain and nearly impossible in the States. Only **Murder at the Open** has been reprinted.

THE HAMMERS OF FINGAL

John Long, London, 1963, 176 pages, 19 cm

Hamish Heathergill, mystery writer of twenty-nine books, and wife Janet, live in Breckadale, on Scotland's west coast. It's a quiet town, but it has its own sinister legend. The action of the ocean waves, washing against the base of the town's sandstone cliffs, has created caves at the water line. When the waves rush into the caves, heavy, muffled metallic sounds, boom up out of the caves. The *old people* say, that in the caves, the blacksmith and his sons are beating on their forges with *The Hammers Of Fingal* and when sparks are seen in the town, someone will die.

Hamish's young prodigy, poet Bruce Cattanach, is in love with Sheena McRae, the barmaid at the Breachadale Arms. He's in the bar when she is man-handled by a wealthy vacationer, McDermott, in town for the golf. Bruce gets overly protective, Sheena gets embarrassed, and McDermott laughs at them both.

McDermott and his business partner, Peter Martin, are discussing golf with the local champion, Collin Campbell, who also happens to be McDermott's cousin. A game is arranged. Collin will play their best ball. A modest bet, (which Collin can't afford) is made on the game. Before going out to play, McDermott, in a confidential conversation, overheard by Sheena, tells Collin that he has made him his principal beneficiary. Collin is his only other relative, and his wife is having an affair with Martin. The match is played and won by the partners on the last hole with a heroic putt by Martin. Martin and Collin walk back up to the club house were Collin pays off the bet, declines a drink because it's getting dark, and drives off. McDermott had stayed on the course to look for a ball he shanked into the burn on the seventeenth hole. As it gets full dark, the Hammers Of Fingal are booming over the golf course into town. Janet and Hammish take the short-cut over the course, back home. Crossing the bridge over the burn at seventeen, Janet sees a body, McDermott's, lying in the water. He's been beaten to death with a golf club.

MURDER AT THE OPEN

Long, London, 1965, 184 pages, 19cm

The author used both himself and his son Jock, also a golf journalist, as characters in this book. The town and the Old Course at St. Andrews are also main characters in the story. The author's affection for both is evident.

Angus and his friend and golfing companion, Professor Aidan Campbell of the University of Glasgow, arrive in St. Andrews for the Open. They arranged accommodations a year in advance, and their room overlooks Score Road, and The Old Course.

The first night in town, they attend an impromptu party, thrown by a wealthy American golf club manufacturer who that day made a hole-in-one on The Old Course. The vacationing pair enthusiastically join in.

Soon after six o'clock the following morning, they walk the Old Course, glad to be on this historic ground and, more practically, as a cure for hangover. Walking up the seventeenth fairway, they head toward the stone bridge over the Swilcan Burn. On their right, is the very deep Road Bunker, and they can see marks in the sand. It is unusual that the grounds crew would miss those last evening.

Angus pokes the marks in the sand with the three iron he carries. He gasps-he has uncovered the closed fist of a man.

The body in the bunker is the American who threw the party. Being the discoverer's of the body and, having assisted the Glasgow Police in a previous murder investigation, Angus and Aidan become involved in this case.

Angus keeps slipping out to the press tent to gossip with the golf writers and then to catch snatches of the golf action. Tony Lema and Jack Nicklaus are the American favorites. The first two competition days, the wind is gale force and the scores sail. Then the wind calms, and Nicklaus goes five under in the first eleven holes.

The weather and the murder occupy the golfers and the police. There is a deadly game of Angus, trying to hide from a pursuer who has a silenced pistol. The chase on a moonless night goes through the castle and, cathedral ruins, up against the sea cliff.

THE PAINTED DOLL AFFAIR

John Long, London, 1973, 184 pages, 19 cm

The Scottish Highlands, the ancient Picts, archaeology, and links golf are presented like a vacation travel brochure, with assassination and, intrigue for spice. Soft boiled with terrific golf sequences.

Like all good newspaper men, Bruce McLintock has informants. Still, he has no idea how to deal with this information from Scliffy Gallagher: Within the next five days, there will be an assassination in the "Village of the Painted Doll."

Mary Jo, Bruce's wife, who has taken classes in Scottish archaeology and the Picts, recently read of ancient stone inscriptions in the town of Pittendall. Say Pittendall fast and it can sound like Painted Doll. Bruce takes the information, minus the informant's name, to Detective Chief Inspector Archie MacPherson, Glasgow Police. Bruce and Archie were boys together in the area of Pittendall and know the town well.

Archie is polite, but not excited by Bruce's information, and Mary Jo's theory about the location. The town of Pittendall is not a gathering place for types who are likely to be assassination targets. Bruce and Mary Jo decide to spend a few days there anyway and, while looking around, get in some golf and write an article or two about the area.

Driving out of Glasgow, they hear the news on the radio about a particularly barbarous murder, just discovered, of the man from whom Scliffy got his information. Something is definitely going on in Pittendall.

When Bruce arrives at the clubhouse in Pittendall, the golf pro abruptly stops his conversation with two Americans. Later, on the course during a friendly game, refuses to discuss with Bruce the event everyone seems to know about but no one is talking about. Bruce continues to dig, and finally figures in the connection between the golf course, and the planned assassination.

McCutcheon, Hugh, British, 1909 - , ***Hugh Davie-Martin***

COVER HER FACE

Rich, London, 1954, 208 pages, 19 cm

There is real tension and suspense in this story. The plot is taut and believable. The golf is great. The Open site and the players' preparations are meticulously described. The intensity of the players, in the final rounds of the championship, and the surprising conclusion of the story, win it a spot on my personal ten-best list!

Howard, is a war hero, whose combat injuries put an end to a possible professional golf career. He still has a two handicap, but plays little, being fully occupied writing detective fiction books and running his own detective agency in England.

On the first page, Anthony Howard saves a beautiful young woman from a suicidal plunge into the Seine in Paris. He calms her down, buys her a brandy, turns his head, and she disappears. Concerned for her, he places ads in the Paris papers, asking her to contact him. She does, leaving a note at his hotel telling him to "pop off." He continues looking for her, and someone tries to kill him.

Following the attempt on his life, he tracks the mysterious lady to England, and the site of the British Open Golf Championship. She is there, traveling with France's hope to win the Open, Charles Rohan, and his whole strange family.

There are nasty rumors surrounding this family of doctors and golfers. They all seem to be involved with the practice of hypnosis, and more than one death is vaguely attributed to their group. Earlier, Charles' lucrative stage career was ruined when one of his hypnosis subjects relapsed into a trance while driving home from the show and was involved in a fatal car crash.

Remorseless, Charles continues to hypnotize young women at parties. Howard connects Charles to a couple of women's deaths, but lacks admissible proof. Then he finds that Scotland Yard also wants Charles. The Yard wants him so desperately that they allow Howard unacknowledged freedom in his investigation.

BRAND FOR THE BURNING

John Long, London, 1969, 184 pages, 19 cm

The author is at his best writing about golf matches, and there are a couple of good ones in here. The story is not his best, but it is not a chore to finish.

Brand Armaments Ltd. develops, and manufactures, new weapon technology which it sells only to countries friendly to England. Lately, someone has been stealing company secrets, and Brand Armaments weapons are being used against England and her allies. Brand Armaments is family-owned, family members hold all the sensitive positions, so the thief is also a family traitor.

Nigel Brand, the adopted son of the company founder, has just returned home from a successful season on the European professional golf tour. His father wants him to give up this "frivolous" life and take his place in the company business. Nigel petulantly proclaims, *ad nauseam*, his hatred of violence and the arms industry.

When one of the company's new gadgets is used to fire-bomb the estate's barn, containing the apartment of the new serving girl, Nigel saves her from the burning building. Although suffering burns and cuts to his hands, he is able to play an exhibition match a few days later for charity. During the match, he spots a spectator smoking the very unusual type of cigarette found at the fire scene. He follows, but loses the man in the crowd.

That night, a security man guarding the Brand house is killed trying to stop a sniper who fired into the new bedroom of the serving girl. Nigel, who is falling for the girl, is incensed and takes to carrying a pistol while searching for the killer. Close to solving the case, he is shot at while driving home one night. Then he enters and wins a professional tournament, and is almost killed at the awards ceremony, by a shooter with a gun hidden in a camera.

McInerny, Ralph, US, 1929- , *Harry Austin, Edward Mackin, Monica Quill*

The author is the creator of three mystery series. Two have been successfully adapted for television. One features a priest, another a nun, and the third a pair of lawyers. Golf is worked into the Father Dowling series, and the Sister Mary Teresa series, at least once. The lawyers in the Andrew Broom series get to play all the time, of course. The author is also the Michael P. Grace Professor of Medieval Studies at Notre Dame University.

LYING THREE

Vanguard Press, New York, 1979, 250 pages, 21.5 cm

Hale, London, 1980

Lying Three is the only Father Dowling title that contains golf, but only a little. A murder on a golf course, and a short final paragraph, in which Father Dowling and the Chief of Detectives make a golf date for the next day. Good story

Father Dowling, assigned to a parish, thinks himself a rather competent criminologist. The good priest is able to indulge in this avocation by virtue of his friendship with Chief of Detectives, Captain Keegan. They enjoy playing cribbage and talking philosophy.

Keegan calls the parish rectory to cancel that evening's cribbage game because of a fresh murder investigation. A distinguished local businessman, recently retired but very active in supporting Israeli causes, has been shot to death on the golf course of the local country club. Recently, the victim narrowly escaped injury in another shooting incident at a Chicago ball game. The Chicago Police classified that first shooting as "random."

Father Dowling asks Keegan to stop by anyway, regardless of the time. When Keegan finally gets to the rectory, knowing he would be pumped by Father Dowling, he is unaware that a former terrorist has been granted sanctuary there. Hidden upstairs in the rectory is a former member of the group claiming responsibility for today's murder.

The story involves illegal arms manufacturing for foreign governments. Characters include a Chicago hooker, a gullible parole officer, and a not-so reformed ex-felon. There are a couple more killings *en route* to the ending. Father Dowling is present at the arrest of the killer.

CAUSE AND EFFECT

Athenaeum, New York, 1987, 210 pages, 22 cm

This is the first title in the author's "Andrew Broom" series. Not much golf, but a promise of more to come.

Andrew is a scratch golfer and has twice been state amateur champion. He wears a Burberry topcoat, handmade imported shoes, and drives a Porsche. All earned from his law practice in the small town of Wyler, Indiana.

Dr. Lister has just given Andrew the results of his annual physical. Leukemia. It is fatal! He is forty-four, married, and without children.

Strangely, it was only a few months ago that he sought out Gerald, his nephew, recently graduated from law school in Chicago. Meeting in Chicago, Andrew convinced Gerald that a junior partnership in his firm and, the position as his heir apparent, were too good to pass up. Gerald's decision is advanced by the knowledge that Wyler is surrounded by high class, rarely crowded, golf courses.

The decision is clinched with a country club membership paid for by the firm, which sports an Arnold Palmer-designed course. In his first few months in Wyler, Gerald's best round on this course is a 79, and he actually beats Andrew a few times, with his handicap making the difference.

Andrew is in a murder trial and doing his best for a client who is making it difficult. Finally, his client is found guilty of conspiring with her lover to hire a killer to murder her husband. There is no longer a chance of Andrew getting her off. Her lover recorded the whole scheme before the killer he hired shot him instead of her husband. The prosecution introduces her dead lover's letter.

From Andrew's perspective, the good thing to come of this trial is a notion of how he might escape a slow death from cancer. Both his parents died by inches of cancer and he will not! He goes looking for a killer to kill him.

If only Andrew knew that Dr. Lister and his own wife are an item, and that the false cancer diagnosis was her idea.

BODY AND SOIL

Antheneum, New York, 1989, 245 pages, 22 cm

The second in the Andrew Broom series starts with the reader's introduction to a killer of multiple victims, busy planning his next, all offered up in the British cozy style. The scene then shifts from the killer's farmhouse to the adjoining golf course. The golf in this series is all the more interesting as we become familiar with the layout of the course at Wyler Country Club. A psychopathic killer operating next to the tranquillity and lushness of a verdant golf course is a fascinating contrast.

Andrew has birdied the long seventh hole, as Gerald makes four and the client, Hal Stanfield, admits to six of the ten strokes he has just taken. Although Andrew is serious about his game, his purpose today is to explain to his client why he declines to represent him in his upcoming divorce. The discussion goes badly, and Stanfield becomes upset.

That evening, in the bar of the country club, Stanfield gets physical with his estranged wife, in front of witnesses. He leaves, and she stays and drinks. He goes home and the next morning is found murdered in his kitchen. The wife is the prime (only) suspect, and Andrew undertakes her defense.

Meanwhile, the mass killer, admittedly lacking certain social skills, develops a relationship with a waitress at the country club where he is a bartender. As victims' bodies accumulate at the farm, this hopeless relationship crumbles and he decides to kill her also. The climax, on the course within sight of the farmhouse, involves the killer struggling to lay Andrew a deadly stymie.

LAW AND ARDOR

Scribner, New York, 1995, 252 pages, 22 cm

Following two titles with no golf to speak of, this fifth Andrew Broom brings golf to the fore. Good golf stuff in this one, including the neat dust jacket.

As this series develops, the Wyler Country Club has become familiar to us, with the expensive homes bordering it and its long seventh hole. This morning three senior club members, pulling their golf bags on trolleys, find the body of Edgar Bissonet, owner of one of the bordering homes, lying in the fairway near the seventh green. Edgar, as usual, is dressed in plus fours, golf shirt, and black and white perforated shoes, and he is clutching a sand wedge.

Andrew Broom is playing directly behind the three older golfers, and they wave him and his partner up. Arriving at the body, Andrew is told by Old Doctor Bullock that Edgar has been dead for some time.

Edgar, a retired investment banker, had turned over his brokerage to his son, and he played golf every morning. He played up and back on the seventh hole, getting in other players' way, but then, he was the wealthiest man in the club.

Edgar's decision to write and publish his life's story had made his wife and son extremly upset with him. He had hired a secretary, young and pretty, while still at the firm and then kept her on when he retired. She was working with him on the book every day, in his home office.

Following Edgar's death, the family find poetry, written by Edgar to the secretary, on a computer disk in his office. It also seems that Edgar was changing his will to provide for her. Then it gets out that the brokerage firm is in serious trouble and will go under without an infusion of cash from Edgar's estate.

The police, now convinced Edgar was murdered, arrest the son. Andrew, the son's lawyer, must also keep the mother from confessing to the killing to protect her son.

While playing a solitary round of golf, Andrew decides that the case turns on the time of day and the order in which the fairways were mowed. The young woman who has a summer job runing the mowing machine is also a scratch player. Andrew arranges a game between them so they can play - and talk.

Manson, Will

A DEADLY GAME

Caravelle Books, NY, 1967, 159 pages, paperback original

There is a lot of golf played in this story, both pro and hacker. The golf is much better then the spying. It is a tough book to find, but it will probably be a real bargain.

Ned Brooks is shy, and polite, and not hardened at all by the experience of spying for five years in Europe with NATO. Earning a masters degree before the army, he speaks French and Russian fluently.

Ned's father, and then his uncle Primus, each died within the past two years, and Ned has no other family. Shortly after Uncle Primus' death, a lawyer notifies Ned of his being mentioned in the will. In the lawyer's office a year later, the inheritance is spelled out: Ned's share of Uncle Primus's estate is two million dollars!

Before Ned gets out of the lawyer's office, he is recruited by the CIA to infiltrate a communist cell in Florida. It is run by Sam Gates, brainy, unprincipled, forceful, and worth big bucks. Lots of money and no real friends! The commies have offered to make Gates one of the rulers after the revolution. Gates lives and plays golf out of the Hibiscus Club in southern Florida. Ned's job is to get close to him and obtain evidence.

Flying to Florida, Ned meets Nancy, a beautiful young lady, also going to the Hibuscus. Both are smitten.

At Hibiscus, Ned hooks up with the Scottish golf pro. To pull his game together, after a five-year layoff, Ned practices secretly every morning. Challenged by Gates one afternoon to a putting contest, he beats him out of a couple thousand dollars, and earns Gates' hatred!

Ned and Nancy pair up in the mixed doubles championship. Gates has won it the past two years and has imported the leading winner on the LPGA tour to be his partner. The match is described, shot by shot, in exquisite detail.

Melville, Alan, British, 1910-1983, William Melville Caverhill
THE VICAR IN HELL

Skeffington, London, 1935, 256 pages, 19 cm

There are any number of tales about the Cliff House at Cheswick. The first owner, its said, threw himself to his death from the big bay windows onto the rocky beach.

It is public knowledge that the Cliff House was raided by police the night of November 17, 1927. Four drug smugglers were accounted for. Two died in the surf of police bullets. However, only one body was recovered. One killed an officer during the raid. He was tried and hanged. The leader, Edward Craig, was captured in the town, trying to steal a get-a-way auto. He did seven years in the gaol.

Seven years later, the Cliff House is now Superior Boarding Establishment, complete with tennis courts and a quite nice golf course. The secret passage from the lounge down to the beach, with an even more secret side passage to an abandoned quarry, have been closed up and forgotten. The golf course was completed without the discovery of the passageway outlet, the quarry having been incorporated into the golf course as “Hell” bunker.

Just inside this secret passages outlet, buried beneath a hastily pushed together pile of rocks, is a small leather bag, nearly filled with precious gems. Mr. Craig, released from prison, is determined to recover his bag of gems. With a full gray beard and quiet manner, he checks into his former home, now the Superior.

Golf, bridge, and gossip are the town’s entertainments. The Vicar prefers golf, checkers, and mystery novels. Dr. Cameron, vacationing at the Superior, has been associated with the police for years. He lends the Vicar lurid mystery novels and is a spirited checkers player.

Playing golf in a mixed foursome, the Vicar fossels a shot into Hell bunker. Hunting his ball, he discovers Sir Horace Hackett, dead! Sir Hackett has been shot, the gun lying nearby. Suicide is the corner’s verdict, but the Vicar is not so sure. He enlists the doctor in his investigation.

The community revolves around match play golf, so it is played and talked about with enthusiasm. A second murder occurs just before the story’s strange, yet satisfying ending.

Miles, Keith, 1940 -, Wales, *Edward Marston, Martin Inigo, Christopher Mountjoy*

It is a wonder that he gets anything written, because this author is always on the go. Being much in demand at Mystery conferences, where his panels are favorites, he is also a playwright and theatrical producer. He has three very different mystery series in production. As Marston, he writes about a Shakespearean period theater company, Inigo has two mysteries featuring a former Olympic track star turned journalist (see **Stone Dead**), and as Miles he has written the following four excellent Alan Saxton golf mysteries.

BULLET HOLE

Deutsch, London, 1986, 217 pages, 21.5 cm

Harper & Row, New York, 1987, 217 pages, 21.5 cm

There is plenty of good golf, including interesting practice sessions in a secluded farmers field. Good story!

Alan Saxton, British touring pro, is getting a little long in the tooth. Too early in his career he won The Open at Carnoustie, creating two persisting problems. Unable to win another major, he is referred to in the press as a *fading star*. Also, due to his fame and stature (6 foot 2 with gray hair), he is easily recognizable.

Alan is so protective of his privacy that, when playing in Britain, he travels and lives in a motor home called Carnoustie. His attitude towards everything smacking of authority is shaped by his father, a career police office who hated golf and belittled Alan as a kid. Now Alan is dealing with a failed marriage to Rosemary and battling constantly with her over visitation rights to daughter, Lynette.

Driving to St. Andrews for The Open, Alan gives a girl a lift. Shortly, he is involved in a minor traffic accident and gets out to talk with the other party. When he gets back in, the girl has disappeared. The next night at his camp site in St. Andrews, there she is, nude and dead in Carnoustie's double bed, a drugged Alan beside her.

Alan does not tell the police everything, out of pure stubbornness. He decides to find the killer and avenge the girl, while practicing for, and playing in, The Open. For help, he turns to Clive Phelps, golf writer for a major publication. Together they decide that the girl's murder is part of somebody's plan to influence the outcome of The Open.

Snooping after fellow pros, Alan gets shot at, twice! His caddie is beaten nearly to death. The wife of an old greens keeper shows him some photos, including some of a group of World War II German war prisoners, working on the course. One of the prisoners in the photo is here in St. Andrews, supporting a German golf star who could win, given the right breaks.

Alan wants to do what is right, but he is difficult to like. Genuine grievances, sound kind of whiney coming from him, but there is no sign of him quitting.

DOUBLE EAGLE

Deutsch, London, 1987, 218 pages, 21.5 cm

Harper & Row, New York, 1987, 218 pages, 21.5 cm

Some very good golf is played. Alan ends up owing the police in a big way! In return, he helps them with the solution. This one has a neat surprise ending.

It is winter in England and Alan is broke. His vehicle, which is also his home, desperately needs repairs. He is overdrawn and does not have his daughter's tuition. Clive Phelps calls and tells Alan of a chance to play in an inaugural tournament at a new super course in Southern California. It is all expenses paid and appearance money. They need a British golfer, who has won The Open, to give this event an international flavor. He will stay at the home of his friend, American golf susperstar Zuke Everett, who has won just about every golf tournament there is. Clive is going to cover the tournament for his paper.

Alan's first surprise is Zuke's new wife, then the new house, then the slipping golf career! Together, Alan and Zuke go to the golf course for a little private party. The architect has made this course so tough, that he offers the pros' a bonus for every birdie or, God forbid, any eagle on the signature hole.

The next day, Zuke makes a double eagle on that hole. That night, at a party in his back yard, he is stabbed to death. When attacked, he is wearing Alan's trademark baseball cap. The two men look much alike.

When the police get there, Alan gets an attitude and withholds evidence. He decides to solve it himself and he starts by visiting Zuke's ex-wife in San Francisco, and hears of drug use, and other activities unbecoming to a sports star. Driving back south, his car is forced over a cliff. Back at Zuke's, he's thrown bodily from the house by the widow's brother, who looks like the guy that pushed him off the road up north.

The police find out about Alan's private investigation, and they are upset, big-time. When the pretty young public relations assistant to the millionaire, who owns the course, is stabbed to death, the police lose their cool. She was on a date with Alan, and the weapon is the same kind that killed Zuke.

GREEN MURDER

Macdonald & Company, London, 1990, 221 pages, 21.5 cm

The golf in this book is the best of the four in this series

Alan's golf game has come back in good form, and he is winning tournaments. Then Rosemary, his ex-wife, notifies him that she is remarrying and that his visitation rights with his daughter Lynette will have to be re-negotiated. Alan is surprised to find that he is upset about both, the impending marriage, and the difficulty visiting Lynette, but he is off to Australia to compete in a prestigious Skins Game.

Arriving there, he takes an immediate dislike to the Aussie tycoon who is sponsoring the game. The tycoon's beautiful wife, a golf fanatic, insists against Alan's better judgment, on caddying for his first practice round. She is kidnapped, right off the course during that round, but not before Alan comes to like her. Before the kidnappers are heard from, there are other practice rounds, with full discussion of the value of a knowledgeable caddie.

Alan's clubs are stolen, and he must find suitable replacements. Then the tycoon insists that Alan be the intermediary with the kidnappers. When Alan gets out of the car to deliver the ransom, the car blows up and kills the driver.

Alan is taken hostage, which reunites him with his clubs and his caddie. He uses his clubs in an escape attempt.

There is an unsatisfying romantic thing with his caddie, and Alan concludes, that he is probably not really over Rosemary. We are left with the impression that he might attempt a reconciliation.

FLAGSTICK

Macdonald & Company, London, 1991, 182 pages, 21.5 cm

Each of the books in this series is set in a different country. The first is Scotland, then the States, then Australia, and now Japan. Toward the surprise ending, there is a deadly golf match, played in the middle of the night on a country club, lit with floodlights. The golf, and the location, combine for an enjoyable read. Where will Alan's next adventure take place?

An extremely wealthy Japanese businessman, who is totally golf crazy, has commissioned Alan to make a golf instructional video, in Japan. At a party, in the man's Tokyo home, he and Alan discuss the project. While they talk privately in the man's study, an explosive device, hidden in the cigar humidor, is detonated and the man is murdered. Alan was across the room when the bomb went off.

Alan regains consciousness in the hospital. He spends a few painful days there, recovering from multiple cuts and burns, but nothing crippling.

Meeting later with the man's four adult children, Alan finds that two of the three sons want the video project to be finished. The third son, who is not in the family business, but a professional golfer of some status, not only does not want the video made, but he demands that Alan immediately leave Japan. The only daughter, a pretty lady, educated in the States against her father's wishes, also says she wants it completed.

However, when Alan is released from the hospital and back at his hotel, he receives a visit from a thug in a suit who advises him in basic terms to forget the project and go home. Ever the contrary person, Alan is immediately determined to stay in Japan, finish the video, and find the bomber, notwithstanding a total lack of knowledge of the language and social customs. Alan is assisted by the video's producer, another pretty, very professional lady who has a nonprofessional motive for completing the work.

The process of making the instructional video, and Alan's tourist experiences in Japan, are absorbing.

Miron, Charles

MURDER ON THE 18TH HOLE

Manor Books, NY, 1978, 216 pages, paperback original

An aging superstar player is challenged by a fresh, long hitting kid, just out on the tour. The tournament, from practice rounds through the final round on Sunday, will keep the reader turning pages.

Mace Brenner has been at the top of the leader board for ten years. In addition to his terrific golf game, he is photogenic and personable. The golf game has accounted for the tournament prizes and they, in turn, have generated endorsement contracts.

All the money, ten years worth of hard work, is invested in a series of business ventures. They are all good solid investments that just need a couple more years of fresh investment capital for them to set him up for life.

The problem is that his game is slipping, and he has not won for a while and needs to borrow more cash for his investments. The existing loans have been renewed a couple of times, and the banks are getting nervous. His biggest endorsement contract is up for renewal, and the ad agency people are wondering, out loud, if he is becoming a little too old to be the spokesman for a kids breakfast cereal.

Mace is quietly getting frantic. If he were still winning, he could deal with the other two things as well: his wife has not been home in a week, and he suspects she might be running with another golf pro; and there is this new, long hitting kid on the tour who looks like one of those that comes along every ten years. He is very, very good!

Mace is up to the situation, and he will do whatever is required to hold his financial empire together. That includes murder, and, there is a murder. It looks like an accident, but a low-budget film crew, shooting something totally unrelated in the area, accidentally gets the killing on film.

Moxley, Frank Wright, 1889-,
THE GLASSY POND
Coward McCann, New York, 1934, 320 pages, 19.5 cm

There are no golf sequences described in this book. There is some discussion of the building of a course using manual labor, and how the workers are treated. Class, sex, and racial disparagement are rampant throughout the book. It is best described as a period piece.

A group of high-rolling executives decide to build themselves a golf course and country club in Suffolk County, New York. It is 1926, and they are riding the business crest. However, in spite of hiring *five old men of golf, ex-golf professionals, seven landscape artists, three engineers, and six independent contractors*, the course is not what they wanted.

They look for a new pro, one who can take over the course and make it playable. The beautiful wife of a member of the search committee tells her husband of a pro who might be available. This pro just happens to be a former college classmate of the couple.

The new pro is hired, and he brings with him his caddie master. He also brings a dark past, a violent temper, and a still-smouldering love for the lady who recommended him for the job.

The committee members, an arrogant group, use their wealth to destroy anyone who happens to cross them. These pre-depression financiers are sure they know all the answers and that the boom will never end. Their arrogance precipitates, in part, the third and last murder in the book. That one takes place *near the opening in the brush by the eighth fairway*.

Moyes, Patricia, Ireland, 1922 -,

TO KILL A COCONUT

Collins CC, London, 1977, 222 pages

THE COCONUT KILLINGS

Holt, Rinehard & Winston, NY, 1977, 222 pages

The specific location of the crimes provides the golf connection, slight though it is. The descriptions of the Caribbean Islands are well worth the reading, and you might want to save this book for a wintry weekend.

St. Matthew's is one of the British Seaward Islands. Recently a neighboring island voted for its independence, but the people of St. Matthew's are satisfied to remain under British rule and protection. Rather suddenly, a group of natives, mostly from other islands, are agitating for a revival of the independence issue. These folks seem well organized, and financed, but the source of their money is a secret.

Things heat up when a U.S. senator is murdered while playing golf on St. Matthew's. He is vacationing at what is reputed to be the most expensive private golf club in the world. Despite rigid security, the murderer gets onto the club grounds, and horribly mutilates the senator with a native machete.

Shortly after, a well-liked young islander is arrested and jailed for the killing. That is when the riots start.

A team of investigators from Scotland Yard is dispatched to St. Matthew's. Their difficult task is to conduct a murder investigation and to convince the islanders that the conclusion will be totally unbiased. They have hardly started when there is a second murder at the club. Another American visitor is mutilated with a machete.

Natsuki, Shizuko, Japan, 1938 -,

THE OBITUARY ARRIVES AT TWO O'CLOCK

Ballantine Books, NY, 1988, 298 pages, paperback original

The author is the leading mystery writer in her native Japan, where this book was first published. Though little golf is played, the book deals extensively with the financing (creative is an understatement) and construction of private golf clubs in Japan.

The story is set in the wealthy suburbs of Tokyo. Two businessmen, both of whom build and market private golf clubs, are murdered. Each is beaten to death with a golf club.

The primary suspect is the landscape contractor for the latest course in which the businessmen were both involved. The contractor is facing bankruptcy because the men had refused to pay for the work his company had performed on the course. A witness heard him in a loud argument with one of the men a few days before the first murder.

The process of financing construction of a new private course in Japan starts with signing a big-name golf architect. Then memberships are sold. It is quite possible to have the memberships completely sold and closed before any work is started, years away from actual play. Members are also required to put up a good-faith deposit which the developers must return, without interest, in five years. The total number of memberships sold is kept secret.

The potential for abuse is obvious. The Yakuza, the Japanese mob, are reportedly involved in selling memberships, with kickbacks from the developers.

Murder is uncommon in Japan, and when the second one occurs, the police are frantic and it is national news. The police procedure is covered in minute detail.

Note: The author has another, so far only printed in Japanese, called **The Lonely Fairway**. Watch for the English translation of this title.

Norton, Olive, british, 1913-, Marion Claydon

NOW LYING DEAD

Cassell Crime Club, London, 1967, 140 pages, 19 cm

This is a small book and a quick read. The golf is near the end, so don't quit, or you'll miss it. The ending is very quirky, with a couple of last minute twists. Stay with it.

Brian Allsop decides to write a mystery. Arriving early to pick up his wife from her evening writing class, he sits down, becomes interested, and makes the fateful decision.

The teacher said that the key to writing a mystery is to select the victim first. Then determine who wants the victim dead. Having a motive, a killer, and a victim, the story almost writes itself.

As his fictitious victim, Brian picks the husband of his wife's best friend, Arthur Hayball. Arthur, the local optometrist, was just elected to the town council on his first attempt. He has no enemies!

Brian spies on him. He follows him in the evenings when Arthur goes to the homes of shut-in's to fit them for glasses. Learning nothing useful, Brian finally goes for glasses himself, even though he does not need them, just to get a look inside Arthur's business. Nothing unusual there except a flashy receptionist. Brian does learn that Arthur plays golf, the same afternoon each week, at his club.

Making an excuse for being there, Arthur shows up at the club. Although Brian has never played golf, Arthur asks if he would like to walk along, as he is playing by himself that day. Brian, delighted, asks if he can pull the golf trolley and act as Arthur's caddie. That agreed, they set on the course. Before the round is completed, one is dead, killed with a sand wedge!

O'Kane, Leslie, US,
JUST THE FAX, MA'AM

St. Martin's Press, NY, 1996, 232 pages, 21.5 cm

Molly Masters, college educated, wife, and mother of two school aged children, runs a business out of her home. She designs custom greeting cards and fax cover sheets. Her specialty is cartoons with a message. In her spare time she gets involved in the murder investigation of a man she despised.

In order to advance her detecting she decides it's necessary for her to go back to high school, posing as the twenty-year-old cousin of her baby sister. It was the father of her fifteen year old baby sister who was murdered. Molly, with the aid of make-up and grungy clothes, drops fifteen years, and mingles at high school. She enlists the help of three pimply faced boys in her investigation.

Her investigation is pointing to three suspects, the men who made up the regular golf foursome of the victim. Learning that they are members of a country club that her husband has a temporary family membership in, she arranges to join their next game. As they play the first hole, she interrogates them, with all the subtlety of a chain-saw in a game preserve. While conducting the interviews, she birdies the first hole. The suspects leave her at the second tee where she joins their wives who are playing just behind them. Molly now interviews the wives while they play the front nine, using the *modified travesty* rules of golf.

The detective assigned to the case, a high school friend, orders her, a number of times, to stay out of the investigation. She gets shot at and an explosive device containing razor blades is left at her home and brought into her by her kids.

Given what you know of her thus far, do you think this woman can be frightened off the case?

Payes, Rachel Cosgrove, 1922 -, *E. L. Arch*

O CHARITABLE DEATH

Doubleday CC, New York, 1968, 191 pages, 21.5 cm

Hale, London, 1968, 190 pages, 19 cm

The golf ball, cap, button, and bloodspot depicted on the dust jacket are all vague clues relating to the books murder and the solution.

The author says that she set this book in Small Town, USA. This is not just any small town; it is a classic company town. There is a new, high-tech company in town, and its management staff are also the social elite of the town. Far Hills Country Club, where most of them are members, is the social center of the town.

The calm of this town is shattered when the body of a mysterious woman is found murdered in a thicket of rough at the Country Club, and no one admits to knowing her!

As the police investigate, member after member, including the owner of the chemical engineering company, are found to have a connection to the dead woman. Most of them are very relieved that she is dead and that they have a solid alibi for the time of death. The police do their thing and, at the company, blackmail, industrial espionage, and company politics race the police to the finish.

***Philbrick, William Rodman, US,* pseudonym of William Dantz**
SLOW DANCER
St. Martin's Press, New York, 1984, 197 pages, 21.5 cm
Robert Hale, London, 1976,

After an exhausting and, unproductive year on the Ladies' Pro Golf tour, Connie Kale is back home. She decides to try something completely different. She is now a licensed private investigator. It is not easy, getting people who know you, either to take you seriously or to trust you with their secrets.

The "Governor", Alfred O'Hare, has many secrets and likes it that way. When his granddaughter Mandy, a girlhood friend of Connie's, is found stabbed to death in the bed of a male stripper, he wants the facts found, turned over to him, and then covered up.

After Mandy's funeral, the "Governor" hires Connie to get the facts, for him and him alone. He also wants, reported to him, the progress of the police investigation. Connie uncovers drugs and blackmail. Before it is over, there are four more deaths.

Connie's dad, Johnny Kale, was a pro golfer, the club pro, and the head greens keeper at Sankaty Head Golf Course, before he retired. He still likes to make golf clubs, and he makes Connie a new set, as a kind of welcoming home gift and, also to try to reawaken in her the urge to go back on the tour. She accepts the gift, and also the sure knowledge, which her dad would never agree to, that she just does not have the quality golf game required to play and win on the pro tour.

In her first outing, with the new clubs, she plays with the current pro at Sankaty Head. While on the course, and discussing the layout, the pro lets out the story of another death. That one was thirty years ago, on this same golf course. It involved the "Governor" and was never solved.

***Platt, Kin*, US, 1911 -, pseudonym of Kirby Carr**
THE KISSING GORAMI
Random House, New York, 1970, 214 pages, 20.75 cm
Robert Hale, London, 1973

The golf is mainly played by the chief suspect in a series of bizarre murders. The suspect is a touring pro, who happens to be leading a pro event, as the story plays out.

Max Roper is a tough detective who has handled some very strange cases. But, this is the first time he has been called on to check out the murder of a beautiful young woman, killed by vicious fish sewn into her gown. The fashion designer, built the fish into the dress, with a little Plexiglas window in the midriff. The autopsy reveals the murdered woman to have been pregnant, and a certain golf pro is her boy friend.

Roper's investigation starts at a pro golf tournament in Southern California, where the pro in question, has a lot on his plate at the moment. He is a former football star turned golf pro, with a reputation for shooting in the 60s on Friday and Saturday, and self-destructing on Sunday. He is also known to be engaged to a beautiful heiress.

Max's next stop is to trace the fish. At the fish store where the designer bought the fish, Max finds the owner with a shark spear in his chest. Moving on to the fish wholesaler who specializes in killer fish, Max finds him with an ice pick in his neck.

Zero for two for the first two stops, Max goes to the local aquarium where the fish experts hang out. He is looking for a wheeler dealer squealer, but he is just a little too late, again. Someone has thrown the squealer in the shark tank.

The story continues with more beautiful women, a Mafia bone cruncher, and a former treasure hunter. All this action is taking place as the handsome pro, losing some of his lead on Saturday, finishes the day with three strokes up on the nearest rival. Finally, there is Sunday, the killer, and the fish.

MURDER IN ROSSLARE

Walker, New York, 1985, 190 pages, 21.5cm

Robert hale, London, 1986,

Though not a lot of golf is played, the course is wonderfully described. There is talk of the type of shot required to avoid a certain bunker or to hold a particular green. The scenes of the small Irish towns, homes, and pubs are an added delight. There is a switch ending, so do not quit early.

Before she died, Katie, his beautiful Irish wife, made Bill Stanwood promise that he would go to Rosslare, Ireland, and visit her sister Noreen. Now retired from the Los Angeles Police Department, Homicide Division, and a recent widower, Bill is on his way to keep the promise.

Noreen has been a bit wild, and moved around a lot, and it takes Stanwood a while to track her down. At a five-year-old address in Dublin, written on the last letter Katie received, he is told that she has probably gone home to Rosslare. He gets there and checks into a guest house.

He inquires about and surprisingly meets Noreen on the fly. She is just running out to an appointment. Her quick hug and promise to come right back for a proper visit is the last he sees of her alive. Two days later, her body is found in the maintenance shed on the local golf course. A bloody five iron appears to have been the murder weapon.

There is an invitational golf match going on at the time, featuring Irish and English high government officials. The next day, while Stanwood is looking over the murder scene, one of these players is shot from ambush.

The local golf pro, and most of the population, for that matter, resist helping the police. Stanwood does not understand the ongoing war they call "the troubles," but it looks like Noreen was involved, and it may have led to her death.

Potter, Jerry Allen, US,

Both of these stories are paperback originals and are not too difficult to find. Nothing on the covers reveals them as golf mysteries, so you have the jump on unaware collectors.

A TALENT FOR DYING

Fawcett Popular, N Y, 1980, paperback original, 222 pages

The sex and violence are graphic, but this is a writer who knows, and likes golf.

The house where Sam Tucker was raised, and his father's blacksmith shop next door, were within sight of Pebble Beach Golf Course in Carmel. It was a natural thing for the young boy to get up at dawn, take a couple of clubs and two balls, and walk over to the dewy fairway. Up and back on that fairway, he would play until the greens crew came out, then home for breakfast and school.

Sam got good, played in college at Berkeley, and won a couple of pro tour events before the Viet Nam war and the Marines. There he lost his left foot, among other things, and spent a few years in a Hanoi prison. In the VA hospital, he got a plastic foot in rehab and an attitude check from Captain Gertrude Summers, Army Shrink. He was walking pretty good on the foot before his discharge, and Captain Gertrude evolved into Trudy.

Back in Carmel, Sam worked on his golf game. The little move he had perfected on the tour, sliding his left foot down and forward an inch or so at the very beginning of the down swing, was where he had gotten so long off the tee. The new foot just did not want to do that move. His swing mechanics were off and they were not coming back.

He would need a new day job. In college, he had done some investigating for Bay Area attorneys, and he still had a California PI license.

In his first case, involving a drug dealing state senator, Sam is beat up, shot, seduced at shotgun point, and nearly drowned, and his home is blown up! But when it is over, Trudy is his new PI partner, and he has acquired a 1928 Bentley to replace his Berkeley era Volkswagen.

IF I SHOULD DIE BEFORE I WAKE

Fawcett, New York, 1981, paperback original, 254 pages

This one is also hard-boiled with everything graphic. There is less golf than in the first one.

Sam and Trudy are back in this story. They are married now, having tied the knot on the Club Nineteen patio overlooking the eighteenth green at Pebble Beach. They have a combination office and apartment upstairs over Ann's Bookstore in Monterey, a nice location. Ann is over seventy years old but not a bit hesitant to help out with her shotgun, if Sam or Trudy, are threatened.

Sam is still trying to regain that little move at the beginning of the downswing, but it eludes him. Thinking about it in bed one morning, he jumps up, puts on his foot, pulls the mattress off the bed and leans it against the wall, drops two golf balls on the carpet, and hits one at the mattress with a driver! It hits dead center and felt pretty good. The second one comes off the toe of the driver, goes through the bedroom window and out into the street. Sam puts the bed back together before Trudy gets out of the shower.

This next case is a San Francisco-area story. A beautiful girl is thrown from the Golden Gate Bridge. She lives! She manages to get to the home of her twin sister, who takes her in. That night, she is murdered in her sister's bathtub. The story involves white slavery, drugs. and some plain old jealous rage.

Sam uses his pro golf reputation to gain access to police records. He cuts a deal with the police detective lieutenant (high handicapper slicer) in charge of the case, who lets him see the files in exchange for a playing lesson on a local public course.

Quiroule, Pierre**, 1892-, Walter William Sayer**

THE GOLF LINKS MYSTERY

Mellifont Press, London, 1935, 160 pages, digest size paperback original

This fragile, digest sized paperback features a wonderful full-color cover. Two golfers, dressed in colorful sweaters and plus-fours, one holding a club, are looking down at a body near the sixth tee.

The title, the wonderful cover, and the fact that the body was found on a golf course are the reasons why this title is included in **The Golf Murders**. There is a single golf shot played in the story, and that shot results in a broken club. The dialogue which is so dated, combined with a number of unbelievable coincidences that dot the plot, actually cause this book to be fun to read.

Because it was only printed as a paperback and is now sixty years old, it is very hard to find. Count yourself fortunate if you are able to acquire a copy.

The book features another period plot in which a bumbling Scotland Yard investigator is set straight by the brilliant, sophisticated, amateur criminologist. The publisher's description asserts:

An unknown man is found lying dead in a well-known Southern Golf Links. He has been killed by a blow on the head by some blunt instrument. The body is naked except for a pair of black silk pajama trousers. There are no footprints near him and no signs of a struggle.

Who is he? How did he come to where he was found, and, above all, who killed him? These are the problems for the police which they prove incapable of solving; and when the hunt is taken up by Doctor Ducane, crime investigator, his inquiries lead him far afield, and through many dangers before the problem is finally answered.

***Roberts, Lee,* US, 1908 - 1976, Robert Lee Martin, SUSPICION**

Robert Hale, London, 1964,

Curtis, New York, 1971, 192 pages, Paperback original

This title has proved to be very difficult to obtain. This annotation was taken from the copy at the Library of Congress. The following is the publisher's blurb.

Suspicion *is the story of a decent man, a physician, husband, and father, who is accused of an illicit relationship* *with a former sweetheart and then murdering her to keep the affair secret. It nearly cost Dr. Clint Shannon his practice, his family, and his freedom.* **Suspicion** *is also the story of Skip Mallory, professional golfer, married to a jealous older woman; of Lucille Sanchez, gentle and loyal nurse who stands by Dr. Shannon; of Chad Beckwith, a policeman torn between duty and friendship for Shannon.*

Other characters move through vivid scenes shifting from Ohio to Florida in a swift story of twisted love, murder, and suspense. Moving breathlessly and inexorably to the final page.

Mallory, the pro golfer, is involved in a tournament in Florida which figures in the conclusion. His play on the final day of the event, complete with a severe case of tournament nerves, is described, shot by shot in graphic detail.

Rocke, William, Ireland,
OPERATION BIRDIE

Moytura Press, Dublin, Ireland, 1993, 337 pages, paperback original

The author's first effort is a dandy, full of great golf. You can see the ball in the air and hear it land. The old caddie knows more little tricks than most pros ever learn.

The British Open is to be played at Turnberry, on Scotland's west coast, and a splinter group of the IRA plots to disrupt the tournament. One hundred and fifty of the world's best golfers, accompanied by wives, girl friends, agents and caddies, TV and press people, and assorted groupies have arrived at the famous course.

The golfers come in private jets and worn-out cars pulling travel trailers; in other words, those who have won and those still looking for, and sweating out their first tournament victory.

Once the practice rounds start, the wives and girl friends must entertain themselves. They come up with a shopping trip to Edinburgh and various other ways to keep busy. One young wife starts her day in the men's sauna, with a handsome pro who has a later tee time than her husband.

The golfers are on the course, hitting shots and checking yardages. For six days, all they talk about, and dream about, is winning the British Open. A win is good for a full year's worth of personal appearances and endorsements for a personable and marketable pro. Wives are expected to stay out of the picture, thank you!

The IRA commander who dreamed up the scheme to destroy, with a bomb, a war monument located on the grounds of the golf course is explicit in his orders that no one is to be hurt. This is to be for public relations only. He really picked the wrong guy to lead the two-person team to pull off the job.

The team leader is a hard-core terrorist, proud of his seven kills and eager to increase the number. His team member is a nineteen-year-old girl whose brother was killed robbing a bank to get operating funds for the IRA. Her father insists she take up for her dead brother.

Arriving in Scotland, the team leader changes the plan and plots to put the bomb under the grandstands at the eighteenth green, set to go off Sunday afternoon!

Ross, Charles, British, 1864 -
THE HAUNTED SEVENTH
John Murray, London, 1922, 320 pages, 18.5 cm

The author, born in India, rose in the army to Major General. He retired in England, joining Shawford G.C., Stoneham G.C. and Freshwater G.C. He contributed articles to Golf Illustrated and Golf Monthly, while authoring five mysteries. The Haunted Seventh is his only golf mystery and it is one of the most difficult to find in the field of golf mysteries. Having access to a copy for only a few minutes, the following narrative was taken from the first page. The dust jacket, very scarce, has so far eluded us.

John Saunderson's narrative: *"You mean to say that he was never heard of again?" "He simply vanished!" Sir Charles replied. "He lunched with me in this very club, in that very room where we have just had tea. He went out afterwards with a few balls to practice, and neither he nor his clubs were ever seen again." "But how very extraordinary," said Maude. "Was his disappearance never accounted for?" "Never! He was presumed to have drowned. That was exactly twenty-one years ago to this very day!" "But," Sir Charles continued, "that was not the only case. Other men have unaccountably vanished both before and since. The queer thing is, however, that these disappearances occur every seven years."*

What an exciting opening, and what a shame that it is so hard to find. This is another that was printed only in England and therefore is going to be quite pricey if a copy comes to market. But somewhere at a flea market or British boot sale, there's a copy priced at a dollar. Keep looking!

Rutherford, Douglas, **Ireland, Pseudonym of James Douglas Rutherford McConnell, 1915 - 1988**
A GAME OF SUDDEN DEATH
Macmillian, London, 1987, 223 pages, 20.5 cm
Doubleday CC, NY, 1989, 183 pages, 21.5 cm

Rutherford wrote numerous mysteries featuring auto road racing, but only this one has a strong golf plot. There is good golf here, both in individual practicing and in the game of the pros. It is also used here as therapy, by a man recovering from a shattering experience. Rutherford knew his golf well, being a member at both Tidworth GC and Aberborey CG.

Patrick Malone played off a scratch handicap at Royal St. George's, Sandwich while he was still in school. From school he had, over a period of years, ended up in the business of chasing international terrorists. There was little time for golf, nor for his family. His marriage, predictably ended in divorce.

At thirty-five years old, seeking stability, he takes a job as head of security for a British oil company. Regular hours and a base in London put some regularity in his life, until Brigadier Jazil, fanatical leader of Kamalia, a middle eastern oil rich country, swears vengeance against Patrick's new employer. Sir Bryon Thomson, head of Royalbion Oil, has cut off operations in Kamalia after two of his employees, a couple, were publicly beaten for a minor civil infraction.

Jazil's first bomb is in the wine cellar of Sir Bryon's country home. The second is found in the parking garage under Royalbion's corporate headquarters. The third is on an oil drilling rig in the north sea, and Patrick is on hand for all the fireworks.

During all this, Royalbion makes a public relations decision to switch its sporting sponsorship from a Formula One motor-racing team to a championship golf tournament. The tournament will be at Sir Bryon's home course, and a member of the Royal family is committed to attend and pass out the awards. Jazil has his own plans.

Shore, Julian

RATTLE HIS BONES

William Morrow, New York, 1941, 315 pages, 19.5 cm

This is another difficult title to find, but luckily it was reprinted in 1944 by the London Publishing Company of New York, in paperback. The paperback edition has the more interesting cover illustration. The scene is the thirteenth green at night. The flag stick, silhouetted by the moon behind, has a skull atop it. The skull is dripping blood onto the green There is a small pile of bones (previously attached to the skull?) on the green at the base of the flagstick. Dated dialog with little golf.

Mark Millner is trying hard to be a tough-guy private detective. He has a loyal sidekick, and he is considered a pain in the patoosh by the local District Attorney.

He has a visit one day from a guy who does not even come all the way into the office to yell at him. The guy opens the office door and stands in the doorway as he threatens Millner. Then he turns and leaves, leaving no name. A few days later, Millner gets a call from the DA, asking him what his business card is doing in the pocket of the body that was found on the Windermere Country Club golf course. The article was in the paper that day:

A horribly mutilated body, which has been identified as that of Edwin C. Smith, prominent businessman of this city, was discovered early this morning by a pair of caddies, in a draw bordering the fairway of the seventh hole of the Windermere Country Club. The caddies, Milton Timms, 16, of 2448 Excalibur Street and Bill Thompson, 19.. .

Millner drives out to the Windermere, the oldest and most exclusive country club in the area. He finds that Smith was not a member, and the caddie-master confirms that Smith had not played as a guest for at least the past month. There is a second murder, and Millner is the prime suspect so he must solve both to get the DA off his back.

Snaith, John Collins, British, 1876 - 1936

CURIOUSER AND CURIOUSER

Hutchinson, London, 1935, 288 pages, 19 cm

LORD COBBLEIGH DISAPPEARS

Appleton, New York, 1936, 309 pages

There is golf from the first line of the first page until the surprising ending. This is a true classic cozy with clues, false leads, and clever twists. The upper-class British dialog of the time is dated, but the story line is fresh and fun.

Lord Cobbleigh, certainly one of the wealthiest men in East Anglia, is fondly thought of by his tenants as a benevolent landlord. Further testimony to his reputation among his near equals is the fact that he is the elected president of his golf club in spite of a lack of skill at the game.

However, his placid world is shaken when he discovers jewels and paintings have been stolen, without a clue, from his manor house. It is almost surely one of the staff, but which one? Lord Cobbleigh is getting on in years, and this unpleasantness is further straining his poor health.

His nephew Dick, next in line for the title and most of the estate, is also a worry. Dick has neither profession, nor job, and he is not looking for either.

One evening, as Dick and Lord Cobbleigh are finishing a late round of golf, a terrible fog rolls in off the sea and across the course. They finish the seventeenth and decide that it is impossible to play the eighteenth. Then the old gentleman finds that he has thoughtlessly left his mittens at the sixteenth tee.

He tells Dick to go ahead and set up drinks. He will get the mittens and join him in the club bar. Lord Cobbleigh never comes in! He disappears without a trace, and the local sentiment is that Dick had done him in and pushed the body out to sea with the tide.

***Steele, Chester K.*, US, pseudonym of Edward L. Stratemeyer, 1862 - 1930**
THE GOLF COURSE MYSTERY
George Sully, NY, 1919, 303 pages, 19cm

Aside from the victim's putt on the eighteenth green, there's only one other golf shot in this story which is replete with stereotypes. There's a black servant, more slave than employee, a French chauffeur who's a *dope fiend* and a fallen lady who says that her former husband should have beaten her because "a woman needs that sometime." The stilted language and the dated plot can be enjoyed as a collection of anachronisms.

Having sunk his putt on the 18th to win his club's championship, wealthy Horace Carwell, collapses and dies on the green. The cause of death is later determined to have been poison but there's a question as to suicide or murder. Colonel Robert Lee Ashley, retired famous detective, is contacted by Viola Carwell and asked to investigate her father's death. Ashley is an ardent fisherman and he would prefer to spend his time reading Walton's "The Complete Angler". She insists, he protests, but finally agrees to take the case. He is still able to get in some fishing, as there is a respectable trout stream running through the golf course in question. The only golf shot, other that the fatal final putt, splashes into the stream just as Ashley is about to land a large fish he has been carefully playing. The ball splashes right next to the nearly beaten fish, startling it into one more surge and its freedom.

Stewart, Walter, Canada,
HOLE IN ONE

McClelland & Stewart, Toronto, 1992, 242 pages, large-format paperback original, 21.5 cm

There is a lot of hacker golf played here, and the slices and hooks are all too familiar. This is a neat story, in an off-beat setting, with interesting and believable characters.

The folks of Silver Falls, a small town near Toronto, enjoy their golf at Boskey Dell. The course was given to the town by a local boy made good, with the understanding that it remain a public course. Now the local Indian tribe is saying that there might be a sacred Indian burial site under the fifth fairway.

Minor harassment of golfers really gets out-of-hand when someone puts a fast-acting laxative in the drinking water container during the ladies' league. The doctored water container diabolically happens to be at the farthest point on the course from the clubhouse.

One day soon after, Old Charlie Tinklepaugh, impatient as always, hits up among the guys on the short par three, and his ball goes in for an Ace! When Charlie rushes up and pulls the flag to retrieve his ball, there is a hell-of-an-explosion and Charlie is killed.

Carlton Withers, reporter for the Silver Falls Lancer, has a plus 20 handicap. He taught the paper's photographer, Hanna Klovack, the game and she is now giving him a stroke a hole. They work together to preserve the course and settle the murders. The second killing is that of an Indian Burial Site expert, brought in to determine the validity of the tribe's claim.

Stout, Rex, US, 1886 - 1975

FER-DE-LANCE

Farrar & Rinehart, New York, 1934, 313 pages, 19.5 cm

Cassell, London, 1935,

There are only a few holes of golf played in this story, but golf clubs and caddies are central to the plot. Stout wrote over forty mysteries featuring Nero Wolfe, eccentric genius at deduction. **Fer-De-Lance** introduced the series and is the only one in which golf plays a role. These books are fiercely collected, and first editions of this title are only seen in special collections; even then, the dust jackets are usually missing.

Wolfe's routine is to sleep late, spend two hours each morning and afternoon with his 10,000 orchids, and spend the remaining hours eating, drinking gallons of beer, and reading. All this is done in his four-story New York City home, which he almost never leaves. Funds for his lifestyle are obtained by solving puzzles, often murder cases, the facts of which are brought him by his right-hand man, Archie Goodwin.

Wolfe is requested to locate an Italian craftsman who is missing after completing a secret commission. The police find him before Wolfe, but, he is dead. At about the same time another death is front page news. A respected college president has died on the golf course while playing a round with his son and another father-son pair. The authorities call it death from natural causes, but Wolfe, and then the recent widow, call it murder. She offers a $50,000 reward, and Wolfe takes up the case.

First, Wolfe publicly offers a $10,000 wager to the local prosecuting attorney, saying that exhuming the body and doing a proper autopsy will prove the college president murdered, by poisoning! Embarrassed, by the wager and even more so by the results of the autopsy, the DA is furious at Wolfe. No praise needed for this master!

Stowell, William Averill, 1882 - 1950

THE MARSTON MURDER CASE

Appleton, New York, 1930, 289 pages, 19.5 cm

There is no golf played, but a golf score card, and a driver kept in a bank vault, do impact the plot. The dialog is quite dated, but the story is interesting and the villain is not revealed until the final page. This is another title rarely seen, but when it is found, the price should be modest as there is nothing in the title or cover illustration to reveal a golf connection. The dust jacket says:

Who killed William Marston? That is what Inspector Burk starts out to learn from the tracing down of clues ranging from a golf score card to the discovery of a secret code, a large withdrawal from the Marston bank account, and a startling situation in the dead man's private life.

Excitement reaches high pitch in the strange disability that cripples the leading witness as the enigma nears solution. Of highest interest too is the contribution of Young, the brilliant and personable handwriting expert, and the delightful romance that lends deep human interest to this challenging mystery tale.

Stuart, Ian, British, 1927 - 1993, *Malcolm Gray*

SAND TRAP

Robert Hale, London, 1977, 160 pages, 19 cm

Sand shots come in for a lot of discussion, as you might imagine. Most pros love this shot, but this story's main character was buried in a sand hill cave-in as a child, and sand still spooks him. The practice regimen of pro golfers is examined in detail.

When three British golf pros who are traveling together arrive back in England after playing tournaments in South Africa, a gym bag belonging to one of them, Doug Scott, is missing at the airport. The following day, Mark Ransome, another of the three, is called by Doug's sister. She says that Doug has disappeared!

Mark agrees to look for Doug, and he first checks in with Peters, the third member of their little group. Uncharacteristic of Peters, he is very drunk and his wife says he has been that way since he got home from South Africa. A few days later, Doug is found murdered, and Mark is beaten when his home is broken into.

Mark attempts to reconstruct events and becomes convinced that Doug had become involved in smuggling uncut diamonds out of South Africa. The missing gym bag apparently distressed Doug's partners sufficiently that they killed him. Now the partners seem to think that Mark knows something of the gym bag, and they are trying to impress him with their determination to recover their property.

Meanwhile, Mark is practicing his golf, especially the sand shot, which he really hates. He wants to be ready for the first spring tournament. Arriving at the tournament site, he schedules a practice round with Peters, who seems sober enough. On the back nine, out of sight of everyone else, a couple of thugs attack Mark. Peters quietly walks off. Mark is buried alive in a green-side bunker, and then....

Tyler, Lee, US,
THE CLUE OF THE CLEVER CANINE
Vantage Press, New York, 1994, 159 pages

This is a first book for the author, who is a travel writer specializing in golf vacation spots. The golf stuff is meaty and well done. The book is short and reads quickly.

The murder victim is killed in her apartment when she surprises a guest stealing a valuable golf collectible from a curio cabinet. It is believed that the killer is also a tenant in the Park Plaza Apartments, because the security is so tight that any outsider in the building at the time of death would have been observed.

The Park Plaza is also known as, *The Dog House,* because it is the only nice apartment complex in town that allows pets. Many of the tenants have pets, and these animals play a role in the plot.

The police investigation team, a young policewoman with a K-9 partner (police dog) and an older male detective, are politically correct in every detail. She is smart and self reliant, he's a sensitive widower, and they both love animals.

She believes him flawed, though not fatally, by virtue of his passion for golf. He uses the rhythm of the driving range as a way of working out mental problems. His habit of thinking in golf terms figures in determining the motive for what appeared to be a senseless crime.

Tyrer, Walter, British, 1900 -
SUCH FRIENDS ARE DANGEROUS
Staples, London, 1954, 224 pages
Garland, 1983,

All of the golf shots in this story are hit in practice. However, these practice sessions reveal a lot about the players. And much more is revealed in the bar of the club house, where the ritual of buying drinks for other members, no matter what one's true feelings are about said member, is strictly observed. A twisting surprise finish caps this delightful story.

The social life of the suburban English town of Beamshott in Surrey is organized around the golf club. The larger homes are on the lanes which border the golf course, and many have direct access to the fairways. Members attending their regular bridge session, or just seeking company in the club rooms, or on the wide porches, often come straight across the course to the club house.

All is calm and pleasantly routine until Ward Pinnock, the painter, remarries following his divorce. The new Mrs. Kitty Pinnock had been his favorite model and is many years younger. She no longer wishes to pose, at least for him, after the wedding.

Kitty busies herself cutting a furious swath through the male population of the club. Members of all ages and social stations are dazzled by her completely uninhibited actions and her beauty. Wives fear, and then fume, when she targets their husbands.

Kitty is found dead in the little pond at the back of her yard. She often bathed in the pond, which is just barely visible from the fifteenth fairway. Very few passed the Pinnock place without looking over the little gate at the pond, because Kitty bathed as she was found, nude.

The scratches on the back of her neck, caused by someone holding her under, brings Scotland Yard into the investigation. There are few mourners but a multitude of suspects. Even the dour Scottish club professional brings suspicion on himself, when he is observed to hit two consecutive slices on the fifteen fairway, with the balls landing near the Pinnock gate, and then making no effort to retrieve them.

Upton, Robert, US,
DEAD ON THE STICK
Viking Press, New York, 1986, 247 pages, 21.5 cm

The author is currently an eleven handicap which he says is ten strokes off his "youthful best". He's at work on a golfing novel, tentatively titled **The Wind Against**.

Consider a beautiful golf course on a tropical island, complete with a high stakes skin game every day, competed for by a bunch of overly mature gentlemen. For balance, throw in a couple of murders on the course, some drugs and voodoo, and a bunker full of deadly snakes. If you've every made a bet on a golf game, you'll like this one!

Amos McGuffin, a mostly unemployed San Francisco private detective, is offered an assignment by one of the City's biggest "white shoe lawyers." This very upper-crust lawyer is a full-fledged golf nut and a member of Palm Isle Golf Club, the most exclusive golf club in the world, located on a tiny island in the Bahamas. The membership is made up of top CEOs and at least one former president of the United States.

The lawyer is one of ten members who hold the mortgage bonds used to finance the club. The bonds are each worth ten million dollars. The lawyer hiring McGuffin is very worried because he has pledged his bond as security for a five million dollar loan, and if he dies before repaying the loan, the lender gets the bond free and clear. The fact that his sailing boat mysteriously blew up at a time when he was supposed to be on it is adding to his fear.

McGuffin gets the job of going to the island, because he once won the area caddie championship, shooting in the low 70's on a tough track. He is to check into the club as the lawyer's cousin, there to just play some golf and get some sun. If necessary, he is authorized to get into the high stakes skin game with members as a way of getting information. Still a single digit handicap, he is looking forward to skinning some of these guys.

Williams, David, Wales, 1926 -,

UNHOLY WRIT

Collins Crime Club, London, 1976, 192 pages, 19 cm

St. Matins Press, New York, 1977, 192 pages, 19 cm

Unholy Writ is the first in a series featuring Mark Treasure, investment banker, and his wife Molly, the terribly successful stage actress. British upper class to the bone, the couple are invited to, or are involved in any number of social events in which murder, not on the program, takes place. The author is a genuine wit, and humor, reminiscent of P.G. Wodehouse, is found throughout.

There is not a lot of golf in this first one, but it is halarieous. Much more is coming in **Wedding Treasure**,

Mark Treasure is asked by one of his bank's valued clients, to help regain the family estate that the client sold during a cash crisis. The new owner is not interested in selling. He thinks there is a priceless Shakespeare manuscript hidden under the estate chapel. The estate grave digger disappears in the middle of a job and is later found murdered.

The new owner hopes to keep his search secret, using the excavation of a swimming pool as cover.

During a break in the action, the new owner (who Treasure suspects of murder) sets up a round of golf on the estate golf course. He invites Treasure, a single digit handicap. One of the construction crew from the pool job is recruited to carry for the owner. The drafted caddie speaks no

Engish and has zero knowledge of golf. The resulting incident on the first tee is a laugh-out-loud sequence of the highest order.

WEDDING TREASURE

Macmillian, London, 1985, 222 pages, 20.5 cm

St. Martins Press, New York, 1985, 222 pages

Good golf and a fun read. The local greens keeper figures in the plot, and he describes, in interesting detail, a number of his tasks in caring for his golf course.

Mark Treasure, and his wife Molly, are invited to the wedding of the stepdaughter of one of the bank's better clients. Guests arriving early are being put-up at a local hotel.

Activities have been arranged to keep restless guests occupied. The evening before, a party is held on the hotel grounds and the abutting golf course. A *closest to the pin contest*, is held on a short par three, even though it is dark and the green is invisible from the tee.

Each contestant is given three marked balls. When all have hit, they walk up to the green to find it covered with balls, and a body! In the center of the green is the warm, dead body of the long-missing father of the bride. There is a wound in his temple the size of a golf ball. What is he doing on the green, and how could a lofted shot, on this short hole, cause such a deadly wound?

On the wedding day, Mark and Molly, staying at the hotel, play a quick nine holes before breakfast, discussing the death while walking the course.

Williams, Philip Carlton, US,
THE TARTON MURDERS

Knightbridge Publishing, NY, 1990, 220 pages, paperback original, bound with *Mission Bay Murder*.

Lawyer turned private detective, Michael Thompson, sat in his living room in sunny California, watching, on TV, the final holes of the British Open. The action was on *The Old Course* at St. Andrews, Scotland, and the players were battling the wind and rain as well as the course. Dirk Maddox, the American was tied with Andy Guinness, the Scot and they were ten strokes ahead of their nearest competitor. Maddox made a spectacular birdie putt at sixteen and Guinness holed out from the bunker to stayed tied. Both had long putts at eighteen. Guinness going first, left his short. As Maddox got set for his downhiller, an old man in a tam, yell an epithet in Gaelic. Maddox stepped away, faced the fellow and yelled, "shut your mouth, you old Scotch fart", stepped back to the putt and stroked it boldly into the hole for the championship. Back in the States a few days later, Maddox, humoring his Scotch caddie, appeared at Thompson's office. The caddie was certain that Maddox was in great danger. Nothing came of the meeting, but the next night someone murdered Maddox with a golf club and dumped his body in a bunker.

The police charged the caddie and Maddox undertook his defense. Maddox and his high-tech sidekick, travel to Edinburgh and the western highlands, getting involved with a ultra conservative, secret clan, who will not stop at murder.

***Wynne, Anthony,* Robert McNair Wilson, Scotland, 1882 - 1963**

DEATH OF A GOLFER

Lippincott, Philadelphia, 1937, 314 pages, 19.5 cm

Hutchinson, London, 1937

MURDER IN THE MORNING

Detective Novel Classic, New York, C1940, paperback

Even though it was written by a Scot and set in North Umberland, the British printing is very difficult to find. The US hard cover is seen from time to time, but rarely in dust jacket. The paperback digest version, sporting a different name is somewhat easier to locate.

The old man, rich enough to have his own golf course, played every day. But even though he could afford all the newest and best equipment, he only played with wooden shafted clubs. That moring, a small group of people were standing around the first tee as he drove off. He imediately fell to the ground, dead. Not visible at first, a small dagger was later found enbedded in his chest. All the weekend guests and their wives had been watching the whole time and had seen nothing amiss. Was the victim fooled into using a steel shafted driver, made to look like wood, which had a secreted air gun in the shaft that shot a dagger into his chest when he drove off?

One of the members of the victim's metal working firm had been experimenting with golf clubs made out of metal of the kind used in making guns

Zimmerman, Bruce, US, 1952 -,
CRIMSON GREEN
Harper Collins, New York, 1994, 327 pages, 24 cm

Besides some excellent tournament golf, the reader gets a look inside the business of golf club manufacturing and the problems of bringing new equipment to market. The business of high-stakes golf hustling is also examined. An MBA is not required.

This year's U.S. Open at Pebble Beach has a very unusual qualifier. Even though he is a highly skilled shot maker, he rarely plays in tournaments, because for years he has been a mob-sponsored high-stakes golf gambler. But, for his own reasons, he is in the US Open, the most important and highly visable tournament in professional golf.

After two rounds, Brad Helfan, longest of improbable long shots, is at the top of the leader board. Then his caddie finds a note in Brad's locker. *Lose big - or die!* Is this just a sick joke, or are Brad's former backers from the mob displeased about the prospect of losing their top-producing golf hustler?

Brad's caddie decides to talk to the mob guys. He earns an introduction to their bone cruncher for his efforts.

The final round is discribed shot by shot and is some of the best golf in all of *The Golf Murders*.

Chapter 3

These Didn't Make The Cut

This section lists a number of titles, each of which has a golf connection which is;

1. So inconsequential that the book does not warrant a full-fledged annotation,
2. Implied but there is none in the book. No other judgment is attached to these titles.

Our only reason for listing these titles is, to help readers and collectors, avoid false trails as they seek golf mysteries. However, the compulsive completest-collector may want to collect them all. There are some dandy stories here.

Most of these titles have one or more of the following:

1. A bloody golf club or golf ball on the dust jacket.
2. A title that suggests golf, for example, **The Country Club Murder.**
3. The title has appeared elsewhere on a published list of golf mysteries.
4. The book contains a map, usually opposite page one, prominently featuring a golf course.

Beeding, Francis

DEATH IN FOUR LETTERS

Hodder, London, 1935

Harper, New York, 1935

Dr. Marjory is very busy in surgery, and unable to join her young man on the golf course, next to her hospital. He makes the best of the delay and practices with his new steel shafted club. *The strident humming of an areoplane* interrupted his concentration. The plane crashed into the course, killing the pilot, and injuring a passenger. While the injured man was being carried to the nearby hospital, a note, suggesting an international military conspiracy, fell out of his clothes and into the possession of the golfer. No further golf.

Berrow, Norman

THE THREE TIERS OF FANTASY

Ward Lock & Co., London, 1947, 255 pages, 19 cm

Three seemingly unrelated scams are successfully completed before the whole plan begins to unravel. The victim in the first, is a maiden lady, who keeps house for her brother, the town doctor. The only bit of pleasure in her life came from her golf. Weather permitting, she walks to the course, plays, and walks home every day. Once she was selected as a victim, the con-man, knowing her habits, arranged to meet her in a secluded stretch of road back to her brother's house. Golf is not mentioned again in the book.

Christie, Agatha

N or M

Collins Crime Club, London, 1941

Dodd Mead, New York, 1941

The war is on in England. Tommy and Tuppence Beresford have to get involved. (They did a bit of spying in W.W.I, you know). Tommy gets a case on the home front, and Tuppence is left home. Tommy unknowningly plays a round of golf with the *number one* bad guy and needs Tuppence to pull him out of danger.

POCKET FULL OF RYE
Collins Crime Club, London, 1953, 191 pages, 19 cm
Dodd mead, New York, 1954,

Rex Fortescue has died at his office, the police suspecting that poison might have been put in his breakfast, go directly to his home. There, they are told that the new widow, as is her habit, is playing golf with a male companion. Two more murders follow but no more golf stuff. A dandy story which regrettably is lacking enough golf to make the cut.

Comfort, Barbara
THE CASHMERE KID
Foul Play Press, Vermont, 1993, 220 pages, 21.5 cm

If you like goats, you'll love this book. It's a murder mystery, right enough, but the plot is all about the goat business in southern Vermont. One of a couple of murders is committed with a golf club. The bloody club, being looked at suspiciously by a bearded goat, is in the middle of the dust jacket. That's it, no more golf.

Crofts, Freeman Wills
FATAL VENTURE
Hodder, London, 1939,
TRAGEDY IN THE HOLLOW
Dodd Mead, New York, 1939

The golf here is in the alibi. No golf is played. The victim's head was bashed in while he searched in a secluded hollow for ancient ruins on the Irish coast. His murderer, wanting to show that he could not have been in the 'hollow' when the deed was done, took some photos of golfers, and —- well - you really should read the book.

Francis, Dick
TO THE HILT
London, Micheal Joseph, 1996, 282 pages

Race horses, of course, but there's so much more here. A young man, living on a Scottish mountain in a crofters stone cottage, without electricity and the facilities, paints golfing scenes for his living. American and Japanese buyers are eagerly waiting. The environmentalists/conservationists want a sword handle from Bonny Prince Charlie (the *hilt* of the title) belonging to his uncle, The Laird. The painter uses his knowledge of golf to thwart their search. Painting, international financial transactions, Scottish history, and decidedly more, with a murder for spice. Great!

Greig, Ian
MURDER AT LINTERCOMBE
Ernest Benn Ltd, London, 1931, 225 pages
Lucky John Swinton (see The King's Club Murder) is just back from his honeymoon and at loose ends. He's recalled by Scotland Yard to investigate a triple murder. The victims were all shot on the same afternoon while guests of their employer. One was hunting rabbits, one boating, and the third playing a solitary round of golf. John and Betty get invited to the manor house and while competing in a tennis tournament, solve the crime with help from an American with a powerful short game. Fast cars abound.

Grierson, Francis
THE BOOMERANG MURDER
Hutcherson, London, 1951, 248 pages, 19 cm

Kate and Miles come into the clubhouse after their golf game. They meet Guy. Both Guy and Miles are very much in love with Kate. The men get into a fight, which is quickly broken up. Kate is embarrassed and Guy, a local policeman is in big trouble, especially when Miles' body is found the next day.

This sequence is on the first page, and that, combined with a map featuring the golf course on the facing page, has resulted in this title being on more then one list of golf mysteries. There is no more golf, but a good deal about the Australian boomerang.

Law, Janice

A SAFE PLACE TO DIE

Walker, New York, 1993

Anna Peters (see **Death Under Par**) and her artist husband travel to Branch Hills, where he will exhibit his work. Branch Hills is a posh, exclusive community, with guards at the gate, and impressive homes featuring state–of–the–art security systems. But murder tries to spoil her husband's gallery exhibit. A fourteen year old girl is bludgeoned with a golf club. The bloody club is on the cover of the paperback edition. There's no golf played.

Maling, Arthur

GO-BETWEEN

Harper & Row, NY, 1970, 204 pages, 21 cm

LAMBERT'S SON

Joseph, London, 1972

They were driving to the next pro tournament when the accident occurred. His wife was at the wheel and she was killed instantly when the car flipped over, he was thrown clear, which saved him. Extensive nerve damage to his left hand indicated, and thousands of practice balls confirmed it, his pro golf career was finished. He became a drunken detective. This title is also on some published lists.

Marsh, Nagio
SCALES OF JUSTICE
Little Brown, Boston, 1955, 303 pages

There has been a murder, in the Chyne River valley at the village of Swevenings. Colonel Cartarette was done in, while fly fishing the *evening rise*, on his part on the Chyne. Murder is simply not done - not in this valley with its old (back to Henry VIII) old families, its private golf course, and its inherited fishing leases on the Chyne. But, one old member, of one of the oldest families, was seen Poaching! on his neighbors fishing lease. Shortly after, the Colonel was found murdered. Oddly, the fatal wound in the Colonel's head, looked like it had been made with a golf club!

Golf plays a part, actually a couple of parts, but sadly their just supporting parts. A very good story, especially for fly-fisher persons. Great fishing dust jacket illustration!

Oppenheim, Phillips, 1866 - 1946, *Anthony Parridge*
A LOST LEADER
Little Brown, Boston, 1907, 296 pages
Ward Lock, London, 1906,

This title has been on all the published lists of sports mysteries. Probably, because the author wrote a substantial number of mysteries, and the pictorial cover shows a wonderful golfing scene. This scene, which only appears on the Little Brown printing, is also repeated ion the frontis

However, the book itself is a novel of political intrigue and romance. There's no crime and only one golf sequence. In it, a mixed foursome get in some mild flirting during a game. The men in suits and ties, and the ladies in the full length dresses of the day.

***Quill, Monica*, Ralph McInerny**
NUN PLUSSED
St. Martins Press, New York, 1993, 216 pages, 21.5 cm

Gregory Doyle, rare book and manuscript dealer, is arrested for the murder of his estranged wife. The Doyles' only daughter, Bernadette, has gone to college on a golf scholarship, and married Augie, the golf coach. Bernie and Augie live on Meadowbrook Country Club, where Augie is assistant pro. The course is near her father's home.

The solution involves the course greens-keeper and the early morning dew. Sister Teresa is pictured on the dust jacket, holding a golf ball.

Ross, Jonathan
A TIME FOR DYING
St. Martins Press, New York, 1989, 186 pages, 21.5 cm

The murderer shoots an iron bolt from a crossbow into his first victim. The second was beaten to death with his own golf club. Combining these two events, the dust jacket designers merged the two murder weapons into one, resulting in a cocked crossbow with a bloody golf club as the projectile. It makes absolutely no sense, but it is certainly eye catching. Of course, there is no golf in the book.

Underwood, Michael
A PARTY TO MURDER
Macmillian, London, 1983, 192 pages, 20.5 cm
St Martins press, New York, 1984,

Lawyers are killing each other off. Midway through the story a couple of conspirators arrange a meeting, on a secluded golf course, in a storm shelter near the second green. The next morning, one of them is found in the shelter, murdered. He has the little directional sign, which points golfers to the third tee, sticking out of his neck. The tee marker, a golf ball, and the bloody sign-stick, make-up the dust jacket illustration. It's a dandy! Too bad there's no golf.

Verron, Robert
THE COUNTRY CLUB MURDER
Wright and Brown, London, 1948, 155 pages, 19 cm

The Manton Country Club is situated on a secluded, and rutted lane, making it a difficult place to follow the comings and goings of it's members. The setting is all-important to the owner, who is involved in wartime espionage, the penalty for which is death! The only game, excluding treason, played at this club, was illegal gambling, carried on in a secret game room. Golf is not mentioned.

Von Elsner, Don (Byron)
A BULLET FOR YOUR DREAMS
Lancer Books, N. Y., 1968, 253 pages, paperback original

David Danning, is an ex-Lieutenant Colonel in the OSS. His government still calls on him for tough jobs. He thinks of himself as semi-retired, playing golf a couple of times a week. On days when his putts are dropping, he toys with the idea of going on the senior tour. This daydream of David Danning is the only golf in this book, but it has appeared on previous published lists of golf mysteries.

Wills, Cecil M.
IT PAYS TO DIE
Hodder & Stoughton, London, 1953, 192 pages, 19 cm

Major Brentwood, falls to his death from the cliffs at Whistling Cove.The map, opposite page one, shows the golf course, separated from Whistling Cove by dense trees. It is possible for a golfer to leave his bag on the course, walk through the woods unseen, and push the Major to his death.

Chapter 4
Short Story Section

Adams, Herbert
THE FATAL ERROR,
The Perfect Round, Methuen, London, 1927

In this collection of short stories, all set on and about golf courses, one involves a murder. **The Fatal Error** contains no golf, but is set at a golfing resort, where a murder is disguised as suicide.

Arlen, Michael
THE BEARDED GOLFER
Ellery Queen Magazine, October, 1952

He was a high minister in the government, but yet, deathly self conscious on the golf course. When he golfed in disguise, wearing the beard, he stopped his slice and cut eight strokes off his game. He had the beard firmly in place, and his golf bag beside him, when he was found dead.

Bentley, E.C.
THE SWEET SHOT
Trent Intervenes, Nelson, London, 1938
Knopf, New York, 1938

A golfer, so universally despised at his club that he must play golf alone or not at all, is found dead on the course. He's badly burned, as though struck by lightning, but there has been no storm.

Bodkin, McDonnell

MURDER ON THE GOLF COURSE

The Quests of Paul Beck, Unwin, 1908; Little, 1910

Vacationing at a golf resort, Beck is drawn into the romantic tangles of pretty Meg Hazel. She has become disenchanted with her engagement to Mr. Hawkins, middle-aged diamond merchant. Handsome young Mr. Ryan has turned her head. When Hawkins is found murdered in the bunker that guards the 17th green, it's Ryan's wedge found nearby that is declared the murder weapon. Ryan is charged and Meg enlists Beck in clearing him.

Christie, Agatha

MURDER IN THE MEWS

Murder In The Mews, Collins, London, 1937

Dead Man's Mirror, Dood Mead, New York, 1937

Hercule Poirot investigates a young women's death. He suspects trickery when her golf clubs, which he observed when he first arrived at the crime scene, are missing the next day.

THE SUNNINGDALE MYSTERY

Partners In Crime, Collins/Dodd, 1929

Tommy and Tuppence Beresford, tackle the case of The Sunningdale Golf Club Murder. A low handicap member, whose golf swing suddenly disintegrated during the middle of a round with friends, is later found dead on the course. He was stabbed in the heart with a ladies hat pin.

THE BLUE GERANIUM

The Thriteen Problems, Collins, 1932

The Tuesday Club Murders, Dodd, 1933

Attending George Pitchard's sickly wife kept him from his golf. Her nurse, Miss Instow, regarded George as quite attractive. When Mrs. Pitchard died, Miss Marple took an interest in the circumstances of her death. Learning of the nurse, she asked, "Is Miss Instow pretty? Does she golf?"

Dickinson, Marguerite

A MURDEROUS SLICE

Alfred Hitchcock's Mystery Magazine, November, 1964

The police were questioning all who played the course the day Dolly Tyler's body was found in the woods behind the caddie shack. That was the day Dan had sliced his tee shot into that area. His playing partner Annie, madly in love with him, couldn't recall him ever hitting a slice before.

Dodge, David

MURDER IS NO ACCIDENT

Esquire Magazine, October, 1949

The regular foursome had finished their Saturday round and were getting undressed to shower. They sent the locker room attendant for a round of drinks. Back within five minutes, he found one of the four, dead on the floor. His jaw was broken and the back of his head caved in. The other three were each in the individual shower stalls and when questioned denied any knowledge of what had happened to their golf partner.

Jones, Bob

MURDER IN THE TROPHY ROOM

Sherlock Holmes, The Golfer, Angel Press, Monterey Ca, 1981

His golfing journal entries for 1890 reveal Holmes' involvement in a murder investigation at The Olde Golf Club near London. The donor of a rare rut iron demanded its return. The Club refused and had a special theft proof display case built to protect it. Despite this, the case was broken into and the club stolen, but the body on the trophy room floor was the man who gave the rare iron to the club.

Kantner, Rob

DYNAMITE PARK

Mike Shayne Mystery Magazine, December, 1984

Jake Borrello didn't want to be seen with Ben Perkins, private detective, so Ben agreed to meet him at North Detroit Golf Club and caddie for him while they talked. Jake was one of those guys who could talk and play golf at the same time. He was running for office, the first time, and there was this women, a former employee, harassing him. He wanted her stopped. Ben said OK, but no rough stuff. Jake offered him Two-Grand to make her go away. Ben reconsidered, then said he'd do what ever was necessary. The first guy Ben sent to see her was shotguned to death in a phone booth right after he had talked to her.

Labrid, C.B.

GOLF WIDOW

Ellery Queen Mystery Magazine, March, 1976

Al played at least nine holes every night after work. His wife started to hate golf the first morning of their honeymoon, when he jumped out of bed for *a quick nine* before breakfast. The occasion of his second hole-in-one was a turning point in both of their lives.

North, John

OUT OF BOUNDS

Cold Blood III, 1990, Ed by Peter Sellers

Mosaic Press, Oakville, Canada

An affair with his neighbor's wife had turned sour and she was threatening to tell both their spouses. Daniel couldn't tolerate a disruption of his peaceful marriage and perfect retirement — with it's unlimited golf. So, he had to kill the woman, using a game of golf for his alibi. He wasn't aware that her husband had a hobby of his own.

DOUBLE BOGEY

Cold Blood IV, 1991, Ed by Peter Sellers

Mosaic Press, Oakville, Canada

He had all the shots to be a touring pro, but lacked the desire to push himself over the competitive edge. His new golf club manufacturing business was at a critical stage and despite his efforts, would probably go under. His partner was draining off what little cash there was. Home wasn't any comfort, with the constant bickering about money. It was ironic that his foursome won a pro-am event that day, because he had a feeling that things would only get worse.

Penecost, Hugh

DEATH PLAYS THROUGH

Ellery Queen Mystery Magazine, September, 1954

Johnny Yale came out on the pro tour with two-hundred dollars, a beat-up jalopy, and a skilful golf game. In a few months the money was gone, the car died, and his golf swing was disintegrating. Duke Merritt, the tour comet, took him on as a protégé and slowly things turned around. With the pressure off, Johnny began to notice the ladies who followed the tour, and especially Duke. The same day Johnny won his first real prize money, someone hit Duke in the head with a ladies' sand wedge, killing him.

Powell, Talmage

IN THE HOUSE OF THE RATS

Ellery Queen Mystery Magazine, September, 1970

The story opens with an elderly man, whose life-time of energy and intellect had resulted in his accumulating great wealth, confined to bed by an accident. As he lays there, paralyzed from the waist down, he contemplates the absurdities of life, death, and the game of golf.

Rambeau, Katherine
ON THE SIXTH TEE
Ellery Queen Mystery Magazine, August, 1969

Buzz and Paula loved golf. Even though their marriage soured and they didn't play with each other any more, they were always on the course with friends. Plans were made for murder on the sixth tee. A good spot for murder because it is completely screened by trees. The hired killer calls himself 'The Harbinger of Joy.'

Rees, Enoch
DEATH BALL
Death Ball And Other Stories
Heath Cranton Ltd, London, 1943

The new caddie master is a stranger and all strangers are suspect, here, on the coast of Wales during the war. The town's war hero is blown-up with a bomb while playing golf alone. Revenge is swift and violent and the golf house will have to be rebuilt. A great period illustration from this story is on the dust jacket and in the color section.

Robertson, Tom
TEE SHOT
Ellery Queen Mystery Magazine, July, 1960

The two business partners were not enjoying their round of golf. For the past couple of holes they had been talking about a very serious, and unaccounted for, cash shortage in the company accounts. Finally the word 'embezzler' was spoken. The authorities would be called in when they got back to the office. The man listening was making increasingly aggressive practice swings when the other man must have backed into his club's path. That was his story, and there were no witnesses, so what could possibly go wrong?

Roos, Kelly

TWO OVER PAR

Ellery Queen Mystery Magazine, January, 1950

Jeff and Haila were having a great time in spite of the bad golf they were playing. At the ninth tee, both sliced their drives into the thicket on the right. In the thicket, they only found one of their balls, and two bodies. Mrs. Carlton and her caddie, Eddie, each shot in the back. The authorities conducted an exhaustive and professional investigation. When it was over, everyone involved agreed that no one had the slightest reason to dislike, far less kill, either one of these individuals. That made finding the killer easier!

Scaffetti, Patrick

A MATTER OF PRACTICE

Ellery Queen Mystery Magazine, March, 1977

She hated golf! Her husband signed her up for a series of lessons and then ridiculed her swing before she caught on. She was determined to learn, practicing until she developed a capable game. Then she beat him, flat out, from the men's tees. And he had yet to see her best shot.

Tilley, Robert J.

THE GREAT GOLF MYSTERY

Ellery Queen Mystery Magazine, February, 1969

His attorney visited The *Fourth Tee Murderer* in his cell, just before the scheduled execution. The lawyer had reluctantly skipped his standing Friday afternoon match, with his regular foursome, to make this visitation. Then, he was glad he had come. He was so profoundly impressed by the sudden and dramatic conversion of his client. Overcome by what the *Fourth Tee Murderer* described, he felt compelled to take the story to the Warden.

Veitterlein, Barbara

DEAR DEPARTED HAROLD

Ellery Queen Mystery Magazine, November, 1952

You could love to hate Harold. Rich and handsome, in a florid, loud, sort of way, he fancied himself the country's most colorful bachelor. Then he met Marilee in her bookstore and fell hard. For a while he seemed changed, but sticky children and smoky outdoor grills became boring. He started criticizing and then ridiculed her golf. He was worse then ever! She took it as long as she could and then left him. He pleaded with her — "Please come back." "One more golf game", she said, "without any remarks about my playing, will be the test to see if there's hope for a reconciliation". Can Harold control his big mouth?

Verner, Gerald

THE FATAL 13TH

The Saxton Blake Annual, No1, London, 1938

The Colonel, Blake's playing partner, teed up, set-up, and drove off. The drive was terrible. Badly sliced, the ball vanished into a clump of trees. Without waiting for Blake's shot, The Colonel snatched up his bag of clubs and set off angrily in search of his errant ball. Among the trees he did find his ball which was lying a few feet from the body of a man, who had a golfball size indentation in the side of his head. Blake, answering the Colonel's shouts, also found another golfball, red with initials on it, next to the body.

Chapter 5

Charts, paperback originals, and index

All of the novel length golf mysteries in Chapter 1 are listed in the following five pages of charts. The charts are designed for easy use as either reader's or collector's guides.The charts are organized alphabetically by book title. Prefix's, such as *a* or *the*, are ignored. Each title is then classified in the following five categories.

Story Type:

By far the most difficult category to assign, due to the high degree of subjectivity involved. The various types, starting with classic cozy, cozy, soft boiled and finally hard boiled could surely be assigned differently, depending on the reading tastes and life experiences of the categorizer.

Golf Played:

Here again, subjectivity is involved, albeit to a lesser extent. The types of golf range from individual practice, through individual play, to friendly matches made up of both same sex and mixed partners, and finally to the men's and women's pro tour. A number of stories could easily fit into more than one category, but one had to be selected.

Sex of Author:

No problem in making selections here, although three stories were authored by couples. Two are by Aaron and Charlotte Elkins and one by the Chabody's.

Sex of Lead (Protagonist):

In a few stories the lead was shared by a couple and these are indicated by the designation *both*.

Setting:

Or, the country where the action takes place. This is not always absolute. For example, **The Limbo Line** by Canning, starts in England, then visits most of western Europe.

AUTHOR	TITLE	STORY TYPE	GOLF PLAYED	AUTHOR	LEAD	SETTING
Christie, Agatha	4.50 from Paddington	Classic cozy	Individual practice	Female	Male	Britain
Chabody, Philip & Flo	The 86 Proof Pro	Hard Boiled	Pro Tour, Men	Both	Male	US
Box, Sidney	Alibi In The Rough	Hard Boiled	Friendly four-some	Male	Male	Britain
Innes, Michael	An Awkward Lie	Cozy	Individual play	Male	Male	Britain
McInery, Ralph	Body And Soil	Soft Boiled	Country club	Male	Male	US
Keating, H.R.F.	The Body In The Billard Room	Cozy	Friendly two-some	Male	Male	India
Adams, Herbert	The Body In The Bunker	Classic cozy	Friendly four-some	Male	Male	Britain
Christie, Agatha	The Boomerang Clue	Classic cozy	Friendly two-some	Female	Both	Britain
McCutcheon, Hugh	Brand For The Burning	Soft Boiled	Pro Tour, Men	Male	Male	US
Ellroy, James	Browns Requiem	Hard Boiled	Country club	Male	Male	US
Miles, Keith	Bullet Hole	Soft Boiled	Pro Tour, Men	Male	Male	Scotland
Dods, Marcus	The Bunker At The Fifth	Soft Boiled	Friendly four-some	Male	Male	Britain
Daly, Conor	Buried Lies	Hard Boiled	Pro Tour, Men	Male	Male	US
Bush, Christopher	TCOT Green Felt Hat	Classic cozy	Mixed four-some	Male	Male	Britain
McInery, Ralph	Cause And Effect	Soft Boiled	Country club	Male	Male	US
Heller, Jane	The Club	Hard Boiled	Country club	Female	Female	US
Tyler, Lee	The Clue Of The Clever Canine	Soft Boiled	Practice	Female	Female	US
Bruff, Nancy	The Country Club	Hard Boiled	Country club	Female	Female	US
Moyes, Patricia	The Coconut Killings	Hard Boiled	Country club	Female	Male	Caribbean
McCutcheon, Hugh	Cover Her Face	Soft Boiled	Pro Tour, Men	Male	Male	Britain
Zimmerman, Bruce	Crimson Green	Hard Boiled	Pro Tour, Men	Male	Male	US
Snaith, J.C.	Curiouser & Curiouser	Cozy	Country club	Male	Male	Britain
Cork, Barry	Dead Ball	Hard Boiled	Pro Tour, Men	Male	Male	Britain
Gregson, J.M.	Dead On Course	Soft Boiled	Country club	Male	Male	Britain
Hamer, Malcom	Dead On Line	Hard Boiled	Pro Tour, Men	Male	Male	Britain
Upton, Robert	Dead On The Stick	Hard Boiled	Country club, gambling	Male	Male	Bahamas
DuBois, William	The Deadly Diary	Soft Boiled	Country club	Male	Male	US
Manson, Will	A Deadly Game	Hard Boiled	Country club, gambling	Male	Male	US
Hamer, Malcom	Deadly Lie	Hard Boiled	Pro Tour, Men	Male	Male	Britain

AUTHOR	TITLE	STORY TYPE	GOLF PLAYED	AUTHOR	LEAD	SETTING
Dexter & Makins	The Deadly Putter	Hard Boiled	Amateur competition	Male	Male	Britain
Bartlett, James Y	Death From The Ladies Tee	Hard Boiled	Pro Tour, Ladies	Male	Male	US
Wynne, Anthony	Death In The Morning	Cozy	Friendly four-some	Male	Male	Britain
Bartlett, James Y	Death Is A 2 Stroke Handicap	Hard Boiled	Pro Tour, Men	Male	Male	US
Wynne, Anthony	Death Of A Golfer	Cozy	Friendly four-some	Male	Male	Britain
Ball, Brian	Death Of Low Handicap Man	Hard Boiled	Country club	Male	Male	Britain
Adams, Herbert	Death Off The Fairway	Classic cozy	Mixed four-some	Male	Male	Britain
Adams, Herbert	Death on the First Tee	Classic cozy	Mixed four-some	Male	Male	Britain
Hamer, Malcom	Death Trap	Hard Boiled	Pro Tour, Men	Male	Male	Britain
Law, Janice	Death Under Par	Soft Boiled	Pro Tour, Men	Female	Female	Scotland
Dunnett, Dorothy	Dolly And The Doctor Bird	Soft Boiled	Country club	Female	Male	Caribbean
Halliday, Dorothy	Dolly And The Doctor Bird	Soft Boiled	Country club	Female	Male	Caribbean
Miles, Keith	Double Eagle	Soft Boiled	Pro Tour, Men	Male	Male	US
Cork, Barry	Endangered Species	Hard Boiled	Amateur two-some	Male	Male	Britain
Duke, Will	Fair Prey	Hard Boiled	Pro Tour, Men	Male	Male	US
Stout, Rex	Fer-de-lance	Soft Boiled	Country club	Male	Male	US
Miles, Keith	Flagstick	Soft Boiled	Pro Tour, Men	Male	Male	Japan
Logue, John	Follow The Leader	Hard Boiled	Pro Tour, Men	Male	Male	US
Durbrudge, Francis	A Game Of Murder	Soft Boiled	Country club	Male	Male	Britain
Rutherford, Douglas	A Game Of Sudden Death	Hard Boiled	Pro Tour, Men	Male	Male	Britain
Moxley, F. Wright	The Glassy Pond	Soft Boiled	Country club	Male	Male	US
Fleming, Ian	Goldfinger	Soft Boiled	Two-some, gambling	Male	Male	Britain
Steele, Chester	The Golf Course Mystery	Cozy	Country club	Male	Male	US
Jerome, Owen Fox	The Golf Club Murder	Cozy	Country club	Male	Male	US
Adams, Herbert	Golf House Murder	Classic Cozy	None	Male	Male	Britain
Quiroule, Pierre	The Golf Links Mystery	Cozy	Country club	Male	Male	Britain
Miles, Keith	Green Murder	Hard Boiled	Pro Tour, Men	Male	Male	Australia
MacVicar, Angus	The Hammers Of Fingal	Soft Boiled	Three-some, gambling	Male	Male	Britain
Hamilton, Patrick	Hangover Square	Hard Boiled	Individual play	Male	Male	Britain

AUTHOR	TITLE	STORY TYPE	GOLF PLAYED	AUTHOR	LEAD	SETTING
Ross, Charles	The Haunted Seventh	Classic cozy	Country club	Male	Male	Britain
Stewart, Walter	Hole In One	Soft Boiled	Public course play	Male	Male	Canada
Potter, Jerry Allen	If I Should Die Before I Wake	Hard Boiled	Public course play	Male	Male	US
Adams, Herbert	John Brand's Will	Classic cozy	None	Male	Male	Britain
O'Kane, Leslie	Just The Fax Ma'am	Soft Boiled	Country club	Female	Female	US
Anderson, W.A.	Kill 1, Kill 2	Cozy	Country club	Male	Male	US
Causey, James	Killer Take All	Hard Boiled	Public course play	Male	Male	US
Knox, Bill	The Killing Game	Soft Boiled	Public course play	Male	Male	Scotland
Grieg, Ian	The King's Club Mustery	Soft Boiled	Country club	Male	Male	Britain
Platt, KIM	The Kissing Gourami	Soft Boiled	Pro Tour, Men	Male	Male	US
Cork, Barry	Laid Dead	Hard Boiled	Country club	Male	Male	Britain
McInery, Ralph	Law And Ardor	Soft Boiled	Country club	Male	Male	US
Canning, Victor	The Limbo Line	Hard Boiled	Public course play	Male	Male	Europe
Daly, Conor	Local Knowledge	Hard Boiled	Pro Tour, Men	Male	Male	US
Snaith, J.C.	Lord Cobbleigh Disapears	Soft Boiled	Country club	Male	Male	Britain
Hutchinson, Horace	The Lost Golfer	Classic cozy	Country club	Male	Male	Britain
McInery, Ralph	Lying Three	Soft Boiled	Country club	Male	Male	US
Knox, Bill	The Man In The Bottle	Soft Boiled	Public course play	Male	Male	Scotland
Hamilton, Patrick	The Man With Two Minds	Hard Boiled	Individual play	Male	Male	Britain
Stowell, William	The Marston Murder Case	Cozy	Country club	Male	Male	US
Dunnett, Dorothy	Match For a Murderer	Soft Boiled	Public course play	Female	Male	Caribbean
Fairlie, Gerald	Men For Counters	Cozy	Public course play	Male	Male	Britain
Fairlie, Gerald	Mr. Maclom Presents	Hard Boiled	Public course play	Male	Male	Britain
Miron, Charles	Murder At The 18th Hole	Soft Boiled	Pro Tour, Men	Male	Male	US
Gregson, J.M.	Murder At The Nineteenth	Soft Boiled	Country club	Male	Male	Britain
Lockridge, Richard	Murder Can't Wait	Cozy	Country club	Male	Male	US
MacVicar, Angus	Murder At The Open	Soft Boiled	Pro Tour, Men	Male	Male	Scotland
Engleman, Paul	Murder-In-Law	Hard Boiled	Country club	Male	Male	US
Platt, Kim	Murder In Rosslare	Soft Boiled	Country club	Male	Male	Ireland

AUTHOR	TITLE	STORY TYPE	GOLF PLAYED	AUTHOR	LEAD	SETTING
Allen, Leslie	Murder In The Rough	Cozy	Country club	Male	Male	US
Brown, Horace	Murder In The Rough	Cozy	Country club	Male	Male	US
Frome, David	Murder On The 6th Hole	Cozy	Country club	Male	Male	US
Christie, Agatha	Murder On The Links	Classic cozy	None	Female	Male	Male
Logue, John	Murder On The Links	Soft boiled	Pro Tour, Men	Male	Male	US
Dickson, Carter	My Late Wives	Soft Boiled	None	Male	Male	Britain
Borissow, Michael	The Naked Fairway	Hard Boiled	Pro Tour, Men	Male	Male	Britain
Adams, Herbert	The Nineteenth Hole Mystery	Classic cozy	Friendly five-some	Male	Male	Britain
Norton, Olive	Now Lying Dead	Soft Boiled	Friendly two-some	Female	Male	Britain
Payes, Rachel	O Charitable Death	Cozy	Country club	Female	Female	US
Natsuki, Shizuko	The Obituary Arrives at 2 O'c	Hard Boiled	Country club	Female	Male	Japan
Adams, Herbert	One To Play	Classic cozy	Mixed four-some	Male	Male	Britain
Gray, Jonathan	The Owl	Hard Boiled	Friendly four-some	Male	Male	Britain
McVicar, Angus	The Painted Doll Afair	Soft Boiled	Friendly two-some	Male	Male	Scotland
Fletcher, J.S.	The Perilous Crossways	Cozy	Individual play	Male	Male	Britain
Kennealy, Jerry	Polo In The Rough	Hard Boiled	Pro Tour, Men	Male	Male	US
Cake, Patrick	The Pro-Am Murders	Hard Boiled	Pro Tour, Men	Male	Male	US
Shore, Julian	Rattle His Bones	Soft Boiled	Country club	Male	Male	US
Fuller, Timothy	Reunion With Murder	Cozy	Friendly two-some	Male	Male	US
Elkins, A & C	A Rotten Lie	Soft Boiled	Pro Tour, Ladies	Both	Female	US
Stuart, Ian	Sand Trap	Hard Boiled	Pro Tour, Men	Male	Male	Britain
Cooney, Caroline	The Sand Trap	Hard Boiled	Country club	Female	Female	US
Bream, Freda	Sealed And Despatched	Soft boiled	Friendly two-some	Female	Male	N Zeland
Adams, Herbert	The Secret Of Bogey House	Cozy	Friendly four-some	Male	Male	Britain
Ferras, Elizabeth	The Seven Sleepers	Cozy	None	Female	Male	Scotland
Kenyon, Michael	The Shooting Of Dan McGrew	Hard Boiled	None	Male	Both	Ireland
Fairlie, Gerard	A Shot In The Dark	Cozy	Friendly two-some	Male	Male	Britain
Hamer, Malcolm	Shadows On The Green	Hard Boiled	Pro Tour, Men	Male	Male	Britain
Greig, Ian	The Silver King Mystery	Soft boiled	Country club	Male	Male	Britain

AUTHOR	TITLE	STORY TYPE	GOLF PLAYED	AUTHOR	LEAD	SETTING
Jardine, Quintin	Skinner's Round	Hard Boiled	Pro Tour, Men	Male	Male	Scotland
Phibrick, W.R.	Slow Dancer	Cozy	Friendly two-some	Male	Female	US
Ingin, Martin	Stone Dead	Hard Boiled	Pro Tour, Men	Male	Male	Britain
Frome, David	Strange Death of Martin Green	Hard Boiled	Country club	Male	Male	US
Tyrer, Walter	Such Friends Are Dangerous	Hard Boiled	Country club	Male	Male	Britain
Gibbins, James	Sudden Death	Hard Boiled	Pro Tour, Men	Male	Male	Asia
Hamer, Malcom	Sudden Death	Hard Boiled	Pro Tour, Men	Male	Male	Britain
Loder, Vernon	Suspicion	Soft Boiled	Pro Tour, Men	Male	Male	Britain
Roberts, Lee	Suspicion	Hard Boiled	Pro Tour, Men	Male	Male	US
Potter, Jerry Allen	A Talent For Dying	Soft Boiled	Individual practice	Male	Male	US
Cruickshank, Chas	The Tang Murders	Hard Boiled	Country club	Male	Male	Britain
Furlong, Nicola	Teed Off	Cozy	Pro Tour, Ladies	Female	Female	Canada
Flynn, Jay	Terror Tournament	Cozy	Pro Tour, Men	Male	Male	US
Devine, Dominic	Three Green Bottles	Cozy	None	Male	Male	Britain
Moyes, Patricia	To Kill A Cocnut	Soft Boiled	Country club	Female	Male	Caribbean
Christie, Agatha	Towards Zero	Classic cozy	None	Female	Male	Britain
Burton, Miles	Tragedy At The 13th Hole	Classic cozy	Country club	Male	Male	Britain
Bently, E.C.	Trents Own Case	Classic cozy	Country club	Male	Male	Britain
Daly, Elizabeth	Unexpected Night	Classic cozy	Friendly practice	Female	Male	US
Williams, David	Unholy Writ	Soft Boiled	Friendly four-some	Male	Male	Britain
Cork, Barry	Unnatural Hazzard	Hard Boiled	Country club	Male	Male	Britain
Knox, Ronald	The Viaduct Murder	Classic cozy	Friendly four-some	Male	Male	Britain
Melville, Alan	The Vicar In Hell	Classic cozy	Friendly four-some	Male	Male	Britain
Bream, Freda	The Vicar Investigates	Soft Boiled	Friedly two-some	Female	Male	N Zeland
Williams, David	Wedding Treasure	Soft Boiled	Mixed two-some	Male	Both	Britain
Christie, Agatha	What Mrs. McGillicuddy Saw	Classic cozy	Individual practice	Female	Female	Britain
Christie, Agatha	Why Didn't They Ask Evans	Classic cozy	Friedly two-some	Female	Both	Britain
Elkins, Aaron & Char.	A Wicked Slice	Soft Boiled	Pro Tour, Ladies	Both	Female	US
Cork, Barry	Winter Rules	Soft Boiled	Country club	Male	Male	Britain

Paperback Original Printing's

First Editions In Paperback

Allen, Leslie

MURDER IN THE ROUGH, Five Start Mystery, NY, 1946, 157 Pages

Borissow, Michael

THE NAKED FAIRWAY, CranbrookGolf Club, Cranbrook, Kent, England, 1984, 192 pages

Brown, Horace

MURDER IN THE ROUGH, Boardman Books, London, 1948, 158 pages

Cooney, Caroline

THE SAND TRAP, Avon, NY, 1983, 190 pages

Duke, Will

FAIR PREY, Graphic Publishing, New Jersey, 1956,

Ellroy, James

BROWN'S REQUIEM, Avon, NY, 1981, 256 pages

Furlong, Nicola

TEED OFF!, Commonwealth Publications, Edmonton, Canada, 1996, 399 pages

Inigo, Martin

STONE DEAD, Sphere Books, London, 1991, 244 pages

Logue, John
MURDER ON THE LINKS, Dell, NY, 1996, 323 Pages

Manson, Will
A DEADLY GAME, Caravelle, NY, 1967, 159 pages

Miron, Charles
MURDER ON THE 18TH HOLE, Manor Books, NY, 1978, 216 pages

Natsuki, Shizuko
THE OBITUARY ARRIVES AT TWO O'CLOCK, Ballantine Books, NY, 1988, 298 pages

Potter, Jerry Allen
A TALENT FOR DYING, Fawcett Popular Library, NY, 1980, 222 pages

IF I SHOULD DIE BEFORE I WAKE, Fawcett Popular Library, NY, 1981, 254 pages

Quiroule, Pierre
THE GOLF LINKS MYSTERY, Mellifont Press, London, 1935, 160 pages

Rocke, William
OPERATION BIRDIE, Moytura Press, Dublin, Ireland, 1993, 357 pages

Williams, Philip Carlton
THE TARTAN MURDERS, Knightsbridge Publishing, NY, 1990, 230 pages

Index